The
Message
of the
Markets

The
Message
of the
Markets

How Financial Markets Foretell
the Future—and How You Can
Profit from Their Guidance

Ron Insana

HarperBusiness
An Imprint of HarperCollins*Publishers*

HarperCollins books may be purchased for educational, business, or sales promotional use. For information please write: Special Markets Department, HarperCollins Publishers Inc., 10 East 53rd Street, New York, NY 10022.

FIRST EDITION

Designed by William Ruoto

Library of Congress Cataloging-in-Publication Data

Insana, Ron.
    The message of the markets : how financial markets foretell the future—and how you can profit from their guidance / Ron Insana.
       p. cm.
    Includes index.
    ISBN 0-06-662045-7
    1. Investments—United States. 2. Stock price forecasting—United States.
  3. Futures market—United States. 4. Bonds—United States. I. Title.
    HG4521 .I38519 2000
    332.6—dc21

                                      00-039588

99 00 01 02 03 ❖/RRD 10 9 8 7 6 5 4 3 2 1

For Melinda

Contents

Acknowledgments

I would like to acknowledge the contributions of many family members, close friends, and others who helped to shape this manuscript and turn a series of anecdotes into a book with a particular point of view.

Art Insana, my brother, provided the research that helped validate the many stories that serve as the load-bearing struts that support the premise of this work. I am forever grateful for his attention to detail and diligence in delivering much needed material throughout the course of putting *The Message* together.

Arthur Cashin provided the impetus for this book by relaying to me many of the most colorful Wall Street stories I have heard in my 16-year career. Indeed, his story about JFK's assassination was the genesis not only of this book, but also of the public speeches I have given over the last many years. The speeches, entitled "The Message of the Markets," needless to say, were the basis for the manuscript.

Doug Crichton and John Bollinger, two longtime friends with whom I worked at the Financial News Network, continue to provide guidance and inspiration and encouragement.

Thanks also to Jason Trennert of the ISI group, for the generous gift of time in helping to shape the manuscript.

Additional thanks go to Arthur Klebanoff, my agent, who took a rather unruly book proposal and used the art of the deal to bring *The Message* to life.

I am extremely grateful for the freedom I have been given by CNBC and NBC to pursue projects like these that allow personal interests and professional growth to be furthered. For that a debt is owed to Jack Welch, Bob Wright, and Ed Scanlon.

CNBC's Bill Bolster and Bruno Cohen are owed debts of gratitude as well for support and cooperation in the development and production of additional television projects that have sprung from the book.

Thanks to CNBC's "Street Signs" staff—Maite Garrido, Andy Hoffman, and Joanne Po—for their input, suggestions, and cover art critiques that proved so useful.

Thanks to Adrian Zackheim of HarperCollins for expressing confidence in this project from the very start. And thanks to Lisa Berkowitz and Michelle Jacob for their tireless efforts to make the book a commercial success.

A very significant debt is owed to David Conti, my editor, who, in a very gentle and evenhanded way, developed this manuscript into an actual book—no mean feat when working with a television journalist. David's constant prodding to make the book better, more complete, and more compelling illustrates why he has great respect in the world of publishing.

Finally, thanks and much love to my wife Melinda and my daughter Emily who have cheerfully encouraged me to complete this work even when it meant my absence from family functions over the last many months. While the phrase "Daddy has to work now" wore thin after a while, there has been no permanent scarring at home, for which I am eternally grateful.

Introduction

It appears that markets of some sort or another have been in existence for thousands of years. There always have been places where buyers and sellers of goods and services have met, exchanged goods, and traded information. That's all a market has ever been, a place to exchange things and ideas. And that's what markets are today. As such, markets serve two distinct but interdependent functions. One, of course, is to facilitate commerce. The other is to gossip about everything else. But oftentimes, the gossip among market participants is well informed and well reasoned. Investors, traders, and merchants often act on that gossip, which ultimately affects the prices of the goods and services sold. In a market, information is the coin of the realm, and so it has always been.

Easily one can still imagine the trade centers of the ancient world, in Rome, in Alexandria, or in the Orient. And one can imagine those worldly travelers who bartered for goods and services, sharing their views of the world, inside stories of palace intrigue, and tidbits of information about which merchant was solvent and which one was going bust.

Indeed, the marketplaces of ancient Rome were quite a bit more advanced than previously imagined. In his eloquently written history, *Devil Take the Hindmost,* economic historian Edward Chan-

cellor breaks new ground in his discussion of financial market speculation in the Roman days. Until only recently, it was widely
believed that the first episodes of speculative excess did not materialize until the Dutch engaged in an orgy of speculation in the
1630s. The Dutch were the first in Europe to build a sophisticated
financial marketplace, where they bought and sold tulip bulbs in
that famous "tulipomania," which some economists claim nearly
destroyed the Dutch economy in 1636.

But Chancellor shows that markets, even relatively sophisticated ones, existed long before that. Roman citizens bought and
sold shares liberally in publicly traded companies. They engaged in
speculation not unlike later episodes of excess. They made and lost
money in a Roman stock market, much as on-line traders do today.

But one can go back beyond even those ancient societies that
shaped modern culture to Sumer, Babylon, and Assyria to find relatively sophisticated, functioning markets. At the very dawn of civi-
lization, there is evidence that the people of Mesopotamia bought
homes with mortgages, exchanged promissory notes, and traded
grain on futures exchanges, much as their modern counterparts do
today. Written documents have been unearthed that prove the fertile
crescent was more than just a simple agrarian culture. Mortgages,
deeds, notes, and other paperwork provide a modest glimpse into
the markets of early days. And while none of those economies of
epochs ago resembles the centers of capitalism today, it is clear that
one of humanity's first inclinations was to organize society around
commerce—and with that organization came markets.

One also can assume that with the constant interaction that
comes with commercial contact, the participants in those transactions shared the vital news of the day, from how the gods were treat-
ing their crops to the physical and economic health of their
contemporaries. Information has always been a key component of
an efficient market, and it was probably no different many thousands of years ago.

Markets clearly have advanced from those ambitious but humble
origins. From the Mesopotamian futures markets to Roman corpora-

tions and from the colorful medieval bazaars to the vibrant port cities of Renaissance Europe and finally to the computer-driven bourses of today, markets continue to serve those two vital functions—to grease the skids of commerce and to transmit information. The information, initially exchanged orally, is ultimately transmitted through the rapidly changing prices of goods, services, and their proxies—tradable securities.

It is that last function with which we will concern ourselves in *The Message of the Markets*. Far more important than how high or low a market goes is the implicit message being sent by market prices themselves. Imbedded in the price of any stock, bond, or commodity is a set of beliefs or a general consensus about value, a consensus that is determined by the careful study of the environment in which that investment exists. It is the cumulative wisdom of investors that determines the price of a good. So, if a stock, bond, or commodity is rising in value, investors must perceive that the environment surrounding that particular investment must be conducive to its value increasing well into the future. Conversely, if investors are driving down the price of a particular investment vehicle, its outlook must have been affected by some known or, as yet, unanticipated event. Most likely the so-called smart money may have already ferreted the news out, well ahead of the rest of the crowd. Legendary market analyst Robert Rhea once noted that markets are a reflection of all knowable opinions and feelings at any given time, a concept that is key to understanding just how useful market messages can be.

In the study of markets, one can find innumerable examples in which market prices turned abruptly, well before the reasons for the turn were clearly evident. But those abrupt turns in the financial markets may contain valuable information about a coming change in the surrounding economic environment. When the price of a stock in the computer industry falls suddenly, seemingly without explanation, it could be a warning that the company has run into an unexpected problem with supply or demand. If several computer stocks fall simultaneously, without adequate reason, it could be that the fortunes of the entire industry have suddenly shifted, though the reason may not yet be clear.

A devastating earthquake in Taiwan in 1999 sent the stocks of computer chip makers reeling on the day of the quake. While the relationship between Taiwan and computer companies may not have been immediately apparent to the lay person, sophisticated investors bet immediately that chip production would be disrupted by the quake. Taiwan accounts for nearly a third of the world's computer chips. The falling prices of chip stocks told the investing world that the quake, which took a tragic human toll, would also have a noticeable economic effect as well.

It is through examples like those that one can see just how valuable market messages can be. Only a handful of individuals recall how the stock market fell in the minutes after John F. Kennedy was shot, *but before* the news of the shooting ran on the newswires. Or how oil prices skyrocketed long before Saddam Hussein invaded Kuwait and months before the 1991 Gulf War was even a remote possibility. Examples like these clearly illustrate how the markets communicate with the outside world, sending messages from which an astute observer can profit.

Frequently, entire markets send signals about the future. Markets are said to be *discounting mechanisms.* In other words, financial markets discount future events by "pricing" likely outcomes into current prices. The price of a stock, bond, or commodity, or the level of an entire market, reflects the future outlook for that individual security, that market, or for that economy as a whole.

Markets may not have been always used as guides to the future. There is scant evidence that markets were used in this way in ancient times, and, only sophisticated investors use the markets in this way today. I know, for example, some very sophisticated investors who will alter their own personal spending habits if they believe the markets are sending a signal of imminent recession. Some will use market guides to time the lock-in dates for their home mortgages. Others try more esoteric personal finance tricks if they think the markets are telling them to do so. I recall a time when one savvy money manager told me about how he was trying to borrow money to buy a house. But he asked the bank to lend him the money in Japanese yen. He believed that the dollar was going to increase in value against the yen. If he was right, and he was at the time, he would have been able to repay his mortgage with a strengthening dollar. As the dollar appreciated in value, it bought more yen. Such a maneuver would have cut his borrowing cost in half over the life of the mortgage. Unfortunately for him, the bank didn't bite.

One can see immediately the value of markets that function in this modern way. The messages sent by the markets can help individuals plan for recession, refinance their mortgages in a more timely fashion, find jobs in a hot, leading edge industry, or simply profit from emerging trends in the stock market.

Additionally, the various financial markets of the world can alert not just investors but policymakers, politicians, and pundits to emerging political and military crises, as we will show throughout *The Message of the Markets.* Most major societal upheavals are preceded by important economic events. The antecedent to the rise of Nazism in 1920s Germany was hyperinflation. The precursor to the Tiananmen Square uprising was a government-induced contraction in economic growth and a vigorous anti-inflation policy. Often, markets anticipate not only the political crises, but the economic upheavals that lead to social unrest.

There are times when markets send mixed, or sometimes errant, messages. Market bubbles represent examples of how the market can appear to be sending positive messages when, in fact, the astronomical run-up in values of particular investments is more a sign of impending trouble than emerging prosperity. Bubbles and their unique messages will be discussed later in the book.

It is quite necessary that the markets being read in this way are free and fair to eliminate the possibility that rigging distorts prices and the messages the markets might be sending. In the case of this study, we will assume, with good reason, that the markets being discussed are both relatively free and fair.

The first portion of the book focuses on historical examples of how markets transmit important messages through their behavior. In the second half of our discussion, we will show how individuals can make the markets work for them, just as savvy professionals do on Wall Street.

Just imagine if the markets could predict when a recession is coming and give you advance warning of troubled times. Would you live your life differently, would you spend less and save more if the markets were foretelling that a recession would arrive in 9 to 12 months? Would an aspiring computer science major in college set his or her sights on the Internet industry in its infancy if the stock market was sending a signal that this was the hottest area of the high-tech world? Would you refinance your mortgage if interest-sensitive stocks told you that interest rates were about to go up, rather than down?

What if the behavior of financial markets could help to identify hot spots in a geopolitical sense? Do increasingly weak and unstable markets offer advance warning of pending political or military turmoil? Indeed they do. Whether it was Germany in 1923 or Indonesia in 1997, markets offered important clues to future political and social decay in both those societies. Conversely, free, fair, and stable markets with steadily rising prices may offer clues about budding improvements in formerly struggling nations.

Markets send advance signals about all these things. Advance information like that can help you make wise decisions, not just about your investments, but about your life. Wall Street professionals have known for years the value of information. As Gordon Gekko said in Oliver Stone's movie, *Wall Street,* "If you're not inside, you're outside." Getting inside requires you to listen to the markets.

The Message of the Markets gets you inside. Of course, not everyone knows how to listen to the markets' message. But we'll teach you how. Once you hear the message, you decide how to act.

1

Wall Street Wisdom

Professional investors know, both in their hearts and in their minds, that markets know things. Markets reflect, as we have said and will say again, the collective consciousness of both astute professional investors and their sometimes less sophisticated counterparts, individual investors. The prices of stocks, bonds, and commodities, as academics will point out, reflect all that can be known about the future with any degree of certainty at a particular point in time.

The academics have given this notion a name: *the efficient market* hypothesis. It suggests that investors make their bets, pardon the metaphor, based on the best information they have at the moment. The prices of investment securities, then, send messages about future outcomes that investors believe to be the most likely.

That is why, for example, retail stocks tend to rally in the months leading up to the holiday shopping season in December. Investors, if they anticipate brisk sales, buy stock in companies most likely to benefit from that year's yuletide trends. Or, that is why the entire stock market tends to fall before an economic recession becomes apparent to the person on the street. Nobel laureate Robert Samuelson, a famous Massachusetts Institute of Technology economist, once quipped that the stock market predicted nine of the last five recessions. And it's true that stock prices sometimes reflect unfounded anxiety about the future. But in the main, the broad movement of markets and individual investments frequently tells us a great deal about events to come.

Investors are paid to anticipate the future. The more accurate they are in their predictions, the better they are compensated. They either win big in the markets or, in the case of professional money managers, are paid better by their clients for being right. It's that simple. Successful investors are successful soothsayers. They can read the economic tea leaves. They work diligently until they understand all the variables surrounding a company, market, or economy. They then make well-educated guesses about the future and hope they are right. If the world doesn't turn as expected, savvy investors often change their minds abruptly and head for the exits. That mass flight from a market can also be quite telling.

Changes in perceptions lead to changes in the values of all kinds of investments. It is those inflection points with which we are often most concerned. For it is that moment when perceptions change that individuals stand to make or lose the most money. Often, perceptions change first among the moneyed class's intelligentsia and then trickle down to the general public.

This book is an effort to help everyone understand that shifts in the markets offer clues to the future. Whether they are small signals that foretell seismic shifts or big shocks that warn of impending calamity, the individual investor needs to view the financial markets in a new and more sophisticated way.

In November 1963, the stock market sent a message of disaster in the moments before the world learned of JFK's fatal drive in Dallas. In October 1929, Wall Street sent one of the clearest messages ever, that the good times would not last. In June of 1990, the crude oil market warned that the delicate political balance in the Middle East would experience a violent and meaningful shock.

Certainly there are times when the markets send errant messages about the future. In October 1987, the U.S. stock market crashed. The Dow plunged nearly 23 percent in a single day. Unlike the Crash of 1929, this crash did not signal an impending recession for the overall economy. But it did usher in a terrible recession on Wall Street. The legendary mutual fund manager Peter Lynch, among the best students of markets and market history, bought more stock the day after the crash. His work showed him that American companies were remarkably prosperous despite the crash. His analysis of the situation proved accurate because he listened to the message of the markets and did his homework. The stock market recovered rapidly even though Wall Street did not.

In the next several chapters, we will examine headline-making events and how the markets sent signals fully anticipating their arrival. Later in the book we will learn exactly how to profit from listening to the message of the markets. First, though, a discussion of some major world events, assassinations, wars, potential conflicts, and other major events that were forecast by movements in the financial markets is presented. Were you listening at the time the markets were talking to *you?*

JFK

The week of November 18, 1963, began as a tumultuous one on Wall Street. It was the week during which the Great Salad Oil Swindle came to a head. And it was the week in which John Fitzgerald Kennedy would die.

The Great Salad Oil Swindle is a little-known scandal of the early 1960s that had huge repercussions in the corridors of lower Manhattan. It is a fascinating tale chronicled by Norman C. Miller, a one-time *Wall Street Journal* reporter, who penned a book of that title, capturing the bizarre story of a Bronx hog butcher who would one day rule the world's vegetable oil market. In the process of his meteoric rise to riches and subsequent fall, however, Tino De Angelis would nearly lay waste all of Wall Street with a deceptively simple scam to corner the salad oil market in 1963. (Yes, Virginia, there was a market for vegetable oil and vegetable oil futures in the 1960s.)

De Angelis, who had made a respectable living as a hog butcher and a fabulous fortune as an exporter of substandard, government-subsidized vegetable shortening to Eastern Europe after World War II, was a short, stout man who eventually became larger than life. His biggest success and biggest failure came in the early 1960s, when he set out to become the global king of oil—salad oil.

De Angelis sprang from humble beginnings, the son of Italian immigrants, who lived in a "cold-water flat of the top floor of a five-story tenement" (1). He was an ambitious young man, anxious to rise rapidly out of the stifling poverty in which he was raised. He worked his way up the ladder at a meat and fish market, managing 200 employees while still a teenager. De Angelis became a hog butcher to the world, something of a legend in New York's meat markets. The remnants of the meat packing district in lower Manhattan still stand today, far less vibrant than they were a half-century ago when New York rivaled the other, bigger agricultural centers of the Midwest.

As a very young man, the diminutive hog butcher started his own meat-processing firm. He shrewdly took advantage of various government programs that subsidized the sales of lunch meat to U.S. schoolchildren or lard to poor, war-ravaged European citizens. In most cases, he was reputed to have delivered substandard products to their ultimate destination. But while he was selling inferior goods around the world, he was living off the fat of the U.S. government. By 1963, he had become one of New York's least ethical business-men, hell-bent on making a fortune using any means possible (2).

His actions in the fateful, third week of November 1963 would devastate Wall Street just as another event that week would bring those five days to a crashing close.

Tino De Angelis was described as an unimpressive figure, even in his heyday. While less than physically prepossessing, he had, however, made some impressive financial gains in his early life. Butchering hogs was his stock-in-trade as a young man. That was a task he attacked with murderous zeal. It quickly helped him over-come the economic challenges of his youth and allowed him opportunities to grow his fortunes legitimately, at least for a time. As his bank account grew fatter, Tino grew too—to a remarkable 240 pounds that hung heavily on his five-foot, five-inch frame (3).

Remarkably, as Tino De Angelis grew in size, he also grew in stature. He built his hog butchering business into an export success, eventually using government subsidies to build a vegetable shortening business into a global powerhouse. True, De Angelis shipped stale and often spoiled shortening to needy countries in Eastern Europe. And true, government investigations often uncovered unethical behavior on Tino's part. But no investigation ever slowed De Angelis down. Nor was he ever stopped from using those government subsidies to sell substandard products around the world.

Emboldened by successes in almost every avenue of business, Tino De Angelis would in 1963 embark upon the most ambitious project of his life.

It was a simple scam that, ultimately, led to great complications for some of the most respected names on both Wall Street and Main Street.

De Angelis attempted an unlikely ruse that, if successful, promised to make him rich beyond even his wildest dreams. His plan was to corner the world's vegetable oil market in 1963. Vegetable oil was a commodity that traded publicly at the time, in a vibrant market, where both the physical commodity sold briskly in international markets and vegetable, or salad, oil futures traded at the commodity exchanges here in the United States.

In an effort to drive up the price of the oil and restrict the supply, De Angelis hoped to make the killing of a lifetime. His scam was as old as any con game ever attempted. He cornered a market by pretending to own more oil than anyone on the planet without ever owning a drop. He managed to stage the corner by filling scrubbed out petroleum tanks in Bayonne, New Jersey, with water. He then claimed that they were filled with vegetable oil, which he in turn used as collateral for business loans. The proceeds of the loans were used to buy up vegetable oil futures contracts on the Chicago commodity exchanges. The ruse gave De Angelis the ability to appear to have purchased nearly all the vegetable oil supply in the world.

By driving up the price of the oil through this scheme, he could sell the futures contracts at an astronomical profit and pay back the loans without anyone ever knowing that he never owned any oil in the first place. (That's not an entirely true statement. De Angelis controlled enough salad oil to fill the testing vials located atop the petroleum tanks. When experts checked to make sure De Angelis had salad oil in inventory, which, remember, was used as collateral for loans, he had just enough to fool the investigators.)

In the minds of most participants, scams such as these could have worked, if there had just been enough time. But eventually the scam unraveled, as scams are wont to do. De Angelis's frantic efforts to manipulate the salad oil market became quite apparent to those who began to investigate his actions. Traders, eventually, bet heavily against De Angelis in the late autumn of 1963.

In the third week of November, prices of salad oil crashed on the Chicago commodities markets. De Angelis plunged into bankruptcy. Hundreds of millions of dollars went unaccounted for. American Express Warehousing, a unit of the venerable firm, also faced bankruptcy. One major Wall Street brokerage house of that time, Ira Haupt & Company, had amassed over $37 million in debts it could not repay, thanks to the loans made to Tino De Angelis's commodity company (4).

Ira Haupt & Company was suspended from the brokerage business in the week of November 18, 1963. It had 20,700 customers who had deposited $450 million in securities with the firm (5). Its suspension led to a small panic on Wall Street in a week that had not yet experienced what a true panic genuinely felt like. That would be reserved for Friday, November 22.

De Angelis ultimately landed in jail. Many firms lost countless millions of dollars. The stock market itself was hurt noticeably by the unraveling scam. Prices on the New York Stock Exchange (NYSE) were under pressure as the companies involved made public their De Aneglis–related losses. It was a nasty week that many veteran traders recall to this day. The stock market averages, like the Dow Jones Industrial Average, were under pressure all week long, as traders and investors feared that the De Angelis collapse could lead to the failure of important Wall Street firms. Indeed, the market did not right itself until late in the week, when the New York Stock Exchange reinstated Ira Haupt & Company and another firm as members.

But if the stock market's terrible price action sent any messages that week, they went unheeded. The rapidly rising price of salad oil in the commodity markets and its subsequent crash should have told some investors that something was amiss in the financial community. Price spikes and crashes, even in rather obscure commodities like salad oil, often lead to wider distress as the impact of the panic spreads beyond those directly involved in the effort. Market analyst John Bollinger points out that salad oil prices crashed before many investors were aware of De Angelis's actions, giving an early glimpse into how markets anticipate events before the rest of the world ever knows about them.

Many of the participants were unwitting accomplices, thoroughly unaware that the man to whom they were lending millions of dollars was nothing but a con man. It is ironic that on Wall Street a financial tragedy like this one, with all its attendant lessons, would be obscured by a greater human drama that had yet to unfold.

Though there was much to be learned from the antics of a scam artist whose conniving ways would become the stuff of lore, it was instead a 10-minute period on a fateful Friday that would send the gravest message of all. That same 10-minute period would provide the greatest example ever of how markets send signals all the time. It was a message that was hard to hear over the din of the moment, but it remains a useful lesson to this day: Markets sometimes anticipate events, or at least send signals of events taking place, that haven't yet reached the general public. Strangely enough, it would be the *stock market* that would say nearly all there was to say about one of the world's most tragic events, several moments before journalists and commentators could make the news known. No more financial panic could send this kind of message. This was a panic of the highest order.

There was an air of cautious optimism on Wall Street on Friday morning, November 22, 1963. The street was still reeling from the aftershocks of the Great Salad Oil Swindle. Several important firms had been threatened with insolvency. Some had gone bankrupt. The principals of many highly respected, white-shoe institutions hung their heads in shame, having failed to realize that one of their biggest clients was just a crook.

But some of the ill effects of the shock were beginning to wear off by the end of the week. Indeed, New York Stock Exchange records show that a sense of calm was returning to the market after an exceedingly hectic week on Wall Street. The price action in Big Board listed stocks was relatively normal throughout the morning. While there were lingering tensions in the wake of the swindle, stock prices moved cautiously higher in the first few hours of trading on the morning of November 22, 1963.

Ira Haupt & Company, the brokerage firm nearly put out of business by its affiliation with Tino De Angelis, was reinstated, along with one other firm, as a member of the NYSE. Investors were working through the financial problems wrought by De Angelis and again starting to focus on bigger issues, like the state of the economy, the direction of interest rates, and the health of corporate America.

The day got off to a good start. Prices on the New York Stock Exchange began climbing from the opening bell. In fact, were it not for the previous four days' events, it would have been quite a good day for the stock market, with the Dow Jones Industrial Average advancing more than three points from the previous day's close.

But just after lunchtime in New York, the stock market began behaving rather curiously. At 1:30 p.m., eastern standard time, the Dow was up 3.31 at 735.96 on volume of just over 4.2 million shares (6).

At just a few minutes past 1:30 p.m., EST, stock prices began to slip. No one knew why. Some traders would later surmise that the repercussions of the salad oil swindle had not yet fully played themselves out. There were worries that another shoe was about to drop. Traders played "rabbit in the woodpile," trying to figure out just which firm would be next to fold as the swindle took an increasingly costly toll on the financial community.

But Art Cashin, a veteran of the Big Board floor for nearly 40 years, recalls those tense moments quite differently. It was, as he suggests, as if those moments were frozen in time—locked in his nearly photographic memory forever.

Cashin witnessed the events of that day firsthand. He remains a well-respected student of stock market history who can rattle off the dates on which many world events occurred with scarcely a break in his mental stride. He can recite Big Board history chapter and verse—from the founding of the New York Stock Exchange under a buttonwood tree in May of 1792 to the day that stock market trading eventually moved to a place called the Tontine Coffee House in the early 1800s.

Cashin's easy facility with names, places, dates, and times has won him great accolades from his colleagues on the floor who view him as something of a living legend on Wall Street. Today, he walks the Big Board floor for PaineWebber, a brokerage house with a long and respectable history.

Cashin's own words describe the scene from that terrible day most appropriately.

I was working in the order room of a small brokerage firm. Our broker on the floor of the NYSE did some brokering for other firms on occasion. [These subcontractors are called $2 brokers since that's the rate they charged many years ago.] At any rate, our floor broker called and asked, "Is there anything out about the president?"

I told him there was no news on the wires and asked what prompted the question. He said there was a sudden burst of selling and that most of it seemed to come from one brokerage firm and that one of *their* brokers said it [the selling] had something to do with the president.

A few moments later the alarm bell on the Dow Jones news ticker began ringing, bringing the first of a series of ominous headlines:

"Shots reported fired at president's motorcade"

(a few minutes later)

"President said to be wounded"

(a few minutes later)

"President taken to Parkland hospital"

(and finally)

"President pronounced dead"

The Exchange halted trading before the final headlines. The sell-off was accelerating as the bell rang at 2:07 P.M., EST.

Like all the nation, we were shocked and stunned. These were the days of bomb shelters and missile gaps. Who was behind this and where might it lead? Those fears had motivated the selling, I'm sure.

But over the next few days of sorrow and mourning, I wondered how that brokerage firm had known or suspected something that made them sellers before the news hit.

The answer, perhaps, exists in a now famous Wall Street anecdote that has been repeated many times over the succeeding decades. It may be apocryphal or a hodgepodge of truths, but it is not just a classic of Wall Street lore—it is an outstanding example of how Wall Street expects you to think and react.

The story goes like this:

The branch manager of a full-service brokerage house told his staff, secretaries, and salesmen they could take a long lunch break to see the president in his motorcade. (In 1963 presidents were not as travel-oriented as today.) The branch manager said he'd stay behind with a skeleton staff—it was a slow Friday, after all.

Anyway, the whole gang came back to the office shortly after he sent them out. "What happened?" he said. "Parade got cancelled!" they said.

Standing at curbside they had seen the motorcade, blocks away, sirens blaring, turn off the route and disappear. As the staff drifted disappointedly back to their desks, the manager showed why he was "all Wall Street."

"Hey," he reportedly called to the salesmen. "Come back here! Give me a bullish reason to call the president out of a parade." A few meek guesses followed.

"To sign a bill."

"To give an award."

But each answer was rebutted with a simple, "That would wait."

"How about a bearish reason to pull a president out of a parade?"

The answers cascaded out.

"A national disaster."

"A nuclear accident."

"A riot."

"An international incident," and so on.

No one even guessed assassination. (They were too far away.)

But he knew 100 bad reasons meant that the likelihood was that the market would go down.

So several minutes before the Dow ran the chilling headline, "Report shots fired at president's Motorcade," one firm was whistling sell orders onto the floor getting prices far higher than those which would be on the tape 15 minutes later.

Art Cashin says that the anecdote taught him a personal lesson—just remember to watch and question! You never know where the things that move markets might lurk—sometimes it's just down the block.

Cashin notes that while he's never been able to confirm all the details of the story, it is a remarkable illustration of how Wall Street demands that one look beyond his or her nose and think outside the box.

Exhaustive studies done by both the New York Stock Exchange and the Securities and Exchange Commission (SEC) say little about how the market behaved between the time of the first shots being fired and the first news report of the event. There was, however, a

10-minute gap between the shooting and the first United Press International headline that ran on the wires.

Cashin was an eyewitness. He saw the selling *before* the headlines and the story is etched in his memory.

In the short time the market remained open after the initial reports were delivered, bedlam ensued on the floor of the New York Stock Exchange. Prices plunged. The Exchange wrote at the time that "the intensity of the 27-minute sell-off that afternoon has never been matched." The Exchange wrote in its study of the day's events that "a minute-by-minute account of what happened on the Exchange in the next 27 minutes would be next to impossible to assemble," though it did manage to draw a "broad outline" (7).

The Securities and Exchange Commission, which also authored a study, notes that panic ensued just after the first reports of the president's grave situation hit the wires at around 1:40 P.M., EST. The SEC says that within 6 minutes, prices on the Big Board started to decline. Mr. Cashin remembers it quite differently.

It is interesting to note that there are no minute-by-minute charts of the market's behavior from that time, as there are today. Few analysts had the patience or wherewithal to construct those so-called tick charts, which plot every move of the market on a graph. Computer technology has ensured that the events of any market event today can be reconstructed with great precision.

The Dow closed the day at 711.49, down 21.16 points. In only 27 minutes, more than 2.6 million shares traded. Had the volume run at that pace all day, the Exchange would have traded 27 million shares, well beyond the average daily volume of 3.8 million shares for all of 1963. In the great Crash of 1929, *only* 16.4 million shares changed hands and that was the NYSE's worst day on record. Today, of course, even individual stocks change hands on much greater volume than that. But in the early 1960s, trading for the entire market rarely topped 6 million shares per day. The cascade on November 22 was swift and severe. The Exchange's board of governors shut the Exchange at 2:07 P.M., EST, 83 minutes early. The ticker tape was running between 13 and 20 minutes behind in reporting transactions. Volume was running at a rate of 100,000 shares per minute, more than five times the rate of earlier in the day.

In short, the Kennedy assassination gave birth to one of the biggest financial panics in stock market history, abbreviated though it was. The magnitude of the decline was smaller than in other previous panics, the Dow fell 2.9 percent that day. That's much smaller than the 5.7 percent decline on September 26, 1955, when President Eisenhower suffered an unexpected heart attack. But both the NYSE and SEC reported that the speed and scope of the Kennedy decline was unparalleled in Wall Street history.

And in the apparent calm before that storm, Cashin's eyewitness account tells us how the market sent a message of impending calamity only moments before the world was aware of what was really happening.

Indeed, for the brokerage house manager who sold ahead of the official news, catastrophic losses were avoided and maybe even a few dollars in profits were protected.

But more important than the dollars and cents is the notion that the market sent an important signal in that 10-minute window. It was a grave signal with the most severe consequences. The stock market itself, which is at the center of the financial universe, showed quite dramatically why it is often at the center of other universes as well.

The markets have always obtained and processed information more swiftly than any other institutions, and it is through this process of digesting and acting on fresh information that markets very often send important messages.

Clearly the markets' abilities to send signals rarely reflect life or death situations, as they did on November 22, 1963. But they often do send important economic information to market participants, investors, traders, and even consumers about upcoming events. There are numerous modern-day examples of how the markets offer clues about the arrival of upcoming events.

One economist on Wall Street told me the story of an unusually observant associate of his who was driving along Steamboat Road in

Greenwich, Connecticut in the summer of 1998. She had noticed a row of vehicles marked "Treasury Department" in front of Long-Term Capital Management's offices. It was a message to her that trouble was brewing in the highly risky world of hedge fund investing. Astute investors know to get their messages from wherever they can, whenever they can. It was an important message about an important, modern economic crisis.

But to fully appreciate the gravity of important market movements today, we must look back on some of the seminal events of the entire century. It is in *these* major market upheavals that we can come to fully comprehend the power of the market's message-sending mechanism. If past is prologue, these stories may serve as important guideposts to our financial future.

The Great Crash

While the stock market flashed a short-term warning of impending trouble in Dallas back in 1963, long before then, in the autumn of 1929, the financial market sent a shocking signal that the Roaring Twenties were coming to a quick and terrible close. There have been countless books written on the stock market's sudden demise in 1929. It was a crash that ushered in the Great Depression. It was the only decline in the history of the U.S. stock market that wiped out 90 percent of the stock market's value in a scant three years. The importance of that crash to the economy has been overstated, understated, and hotly debated by economists, market gurus, and financial journalists for 70 years. The only conclusion reached by the consensus is that the crash was an important market event that nearly everyone fears will make a return visit to Wall Street someday soon.

But the Crash of 1929, whether it precipitated a depression, sent the clearest message a market ever sent: Something wicked was coming this way, something that no American had ever seen before. It was the most stark and visible example in U.S. history of how markets can foretell the future. The stunning plunge of 1929 was worse than the worst of the panics that gripped Wall Street from time to time, such as in the 1870s or even the panic of 1907. (In that panic, J.P. Morgan rescued the stock market with a huge infusion of cash and prevented a panic from turning into an economy-altering crash.) But the "great" crash was no mere panic. It wiped out countless billions of dollars in accumulated wealth and turned the Roaring Twenties into the Tragic Thirties.

But while the crash clearly signaled the coming of the Great Depression to historians who saw the period with the clarity normally associated with 20/20 hindsight, the meaning of the crash was not so obvious at the time. Indeed, President Herbert Hoover, a man somewhat unfairly maligned for his alleged role in exacerbating the Depression, remarked on the day of the crash that the economy was "fundamentally sound." Those words would have a hollow ring to them only a few short months after the market's historic plunge.

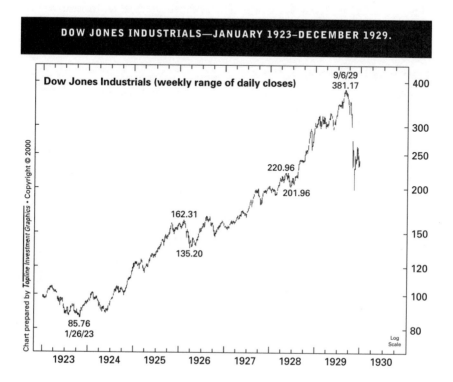

DOW JONES INDUSTRIALS—JANUARY 1923–DECEMBER 1929.

Dow Jones Industrials (weekly range of daily closes)

9/6/29
381.17

400

300

250

220.96

201.96

200

162.31

150

135.20

120

100

85.76
1/26/23

80

Log Scale

Chart prepared by *Topline Investment Graphics* • Copyright © 2000

1923 1924 1925 1926 1927 1928 1929 1930

The heady days of the Roaring Twenties were, in some ways, very much like the current market and economic environment. New technologies were rapidly changing the pace of economic change, boosting worker productivity, and giving rise to entirely new ways of doing business.

The auto industry was maturing, forever altering every facet of American life, from methods of industrial production to the modes of domestic transportation. In many ways, the advent of the car was even more important to the American way of life than the advent of the personal computer. Its introduction led to a wholesale change in the composition of the U.S. economy, shifting productive resources from the agricultural sector to the quickly burgeoning manufacturing sector. Today, the computer and the Internet have quickly taken the U.S. economy from the industrial age to the information age, with greater speed and an even greater likelihood of dislocation for those not able to adapt to the fast changing world of the new economy.

The 1920s also saw the greatest bull market in the history of Wall Street. The Dow Jones Industrial Average rose from below 100 in 1923 to a high of 381 in September of 1929, a better than 350 percent gain. It is a gain that is still unmatched by the great bull market of the 1990s.

Money was easy. Business boomed. Real estate values skyrocketed from Wall Street to Palm Beach. And everyone should have gotten rich, as industrialist John Jacob Raskob suggested in the *Ladies' Home Journal* in 1928. The U.S. enjoyed an embarrassment of riches in those Gatsby days, or at least it seemed so for a time.

But while the rich got richer, ominous signs were appearing on the economic horizon—signs that went unnoticed by the population at large. Maybe it was because economic data were collected more slowly or disseminated more discreetly. Maybe people were enjoying themselves too much to notice the worrisome developments all around them. In any case, the small but important warning signs that cropped up throughout the mid-1920s would be thoroughly overshadowed by a market message that was far too obvious to ignore.

Before the stock market plunged in October 1929, the events of previous years merit some consideration, since they sent the early warning signs that not all Americans were sipping champagne from someone's slipper.

Throughout the entire decade of the 1920s, an average of 600 banks failed every year. The value of farmland declined 30 to 40 percent between 1920 and 1929. By 1929, the richest 1 percent of the population controlled 40 percent of the nation's wealth, while the bottom 93 percent saw their incomes fall 4 percent between 1923 and 1929 (8). The much-vaunted Roaring Twenties roared for only the urban elite, certainly not for the great masses, many of whom earned subsistence wages back on the farm.

The playing field would be leveled in the autumn of 1929. The stock market crash began on October 24, culminating in crushing back-to-back 12 percent declines on the 28th and 29th of the month. The declines on Monday and Black Tuesday of that terrible week would slash the stock market's value by over 20 percent. In October alone, losses on Wall Street would top $16 billion, a catastrophic loss of market value in those days (9).

The declines would grow even more punishing in the next few years, sending a signal from Wall Street to Main Street that this was no ordinary recession.

In the two months prior to the crash, industrial production declined at a 20 percent annual rate. Auto sales peaked well before the stock market's troubles. Those were two very early warning signs that the economy and stock market were out of sync. Wholesale prices plunged 7.5 percent, ushering in the great deflation of the 1930s. Personal incomes contracted by 5 percent in that period.

The U.S. economy would not suffer such staggeringly large losses again in the century.

The market's meltdown both coincided with, and foretold of, even darker days to come. From its peak of 381 in 1929, the Dow would plummet to a low of 41 in July of 1932. The Dow hadn't touched a level that low since 1896 when it was first calculated by financial journalist Charles Dow and his partner, Mr. Jones.

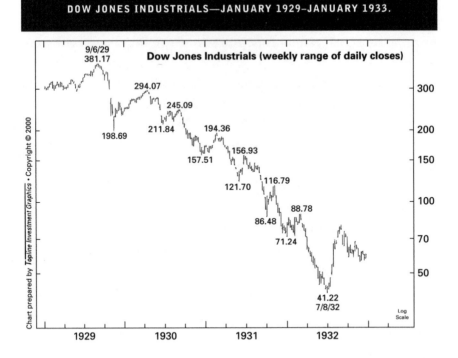

Wall Street's worst fears about Main Street were quickly realized. In 1930, the nation's gross national product (GNP) contracted at an eye-popping 9.4 percent annual rate. The unemployment rate surged, more than doubling from a low of 3.2 percent to 8.7 percent. The nation's GNP fell another 8.5 percent in 1931, while the unemployment rate exploded to nearly 16 percent (10).

But that would not represent the worst that the Great Depression had to offer. Consider the following statistics from 1932:

GNP shrinks by a record 13.4 percent.

The unemployment rate hits a record 23.6 percent.

Ten thousand or 40 percent of all U.S. banks fail.

Farm prices plunge 53 percent since 1929.

International trade collapses by 66 percent (11).

As we all know from our history lessons, the Depression caused millions of Americans to suffer great hardships. The very fabric of American society was tattered and torn. The government of Herbert

Hoover was drummed out of office. Franklin D. Roosevelt was swept into the White House by a population suddenly fearful of the future. Many of the most downtrodden and disillusioned citizens flirted with socialism and communism. By 1932, the masses had grown so restive that Douglas MacArthur, whose star was on the rise, was dispatched to break up the famous Veteran's Bonus March in 1932. The future army hero was expected to cleanse the "awful stench of revolution" that hung in the air at the Great Depression's low point.

It would ultimately take a world war and subsequent rebuilding boom to erase those haunting images of dust bowls, of breadlines, and of poverty from the national psyche.

The Crash of 1929 was the most ominous message the markets ever sent and one that still strikes fear into the heart of any student of stock market history.

Almost exactly after six decades passed, the markets would witness another crash, this one more terrible than the first. On October 19, 1987, the Dow Jones Industrial Average would suffer its biggest drop ever, sending shock waves up and down Wall Street. Having stood on the floor of a major Chicago futures exchange on that day of reckoning, I vividly recall the terror of the moment. Veteran investors were shell-shocked. Young investors dropped out of the game right in front of my eyes. Traders literally trembled at the end of an excruciating day, terrified that their careers were coming to a rapid conclusion. Policymakers scrambled to respond. Regulators frantically searched for reasons to explain such a precipitous and ominous decline.

The world watched in horror that day, as a most welcome period of prosperity was visibly threatened by the invisible hand of the market.

But unlike 1929, the message of the market in 1987 was quite different. That crash affected Wall Street for years. But in many ways, the crash of 1987 lent Main Street a helping hand. It forced many important changes that set the stage for renewed prosperity in the decade that followed. Again, the market told us how and why long before such facts were obvious to us all.

The Other Crash

October 19, 1987 is a day that will forever live in infamy on Wall Street. It was the day on which the Dow Jones Industrial Average suffered its biggest one-day loss in history. The staggering 508-point plunge was not just the single biggest point drop ever, it was the largest one-day percentage decline ever recorded on Wall Street. The ferocious descent wiped out 22.7 percent of the market's value in six and one-half hours. Only the back-to-back declines on October 28 and October 29 of 1929 rivaled the Dow's losses that day.

As was the case in 1929, there were plenty of signs of impending disaster on Wall Street that year. But unlike 1929, the market's ultimate message was far different in the late 1980s than in the late 1920s.

The history of the 1987 crash was written almost immediately after the event itself. Nobel laureate Merton Miller authored a study of the crash through the University of Chicago. The *Wall Street Journal's* Tim Metz turned out an instant book on the crash entitled *Black Monday,* which clearly chronicled the events surrounding the market's unprecedented meltdown.

The crash of 1987 was a complicated event that had great meaning for Wall Street and very little meaning for Main Street. Given the public's lack of exposure to stock market investments in the 1980s, it was no wonder the "man on the street" ignored the market's swoon, while the men and women of Wall Street immediately panicked about their futures.

Various accounts of the crash identified different causes and predicted different outcomes in the wake of the event. What they failed to do, however, in large part was to show how the markets themselves were sending clear messages that a calamity was in the making and that it was time to pay the market heed.

The great bull market of the 1980s started rather inauspiciously in the summer of 1982, when the Dow reached a low of 774. Stocks had been undergoing years of dramatic swings since 1968 when the Dow topped out at 1000. It was a millennial mark that would not be meaningfully broken for nearly 16 years.

Through the crushing bear markets in 1973 and 1974 to repeat "October massacres" of 1978 and 1979, stock investors suffered for years as inflation and rising interest rates sharply reduced the value of financial assets. The twin oil shocks of the 1970s, the lingering effects of the Vietnam War, the erratic economic policies of Presidents Nixon, Ford, and Carter made Wall Street and Main Street anything but the easy streets of the 1950s and 1960s.

But all of that quietly changed in August 1982. Ronald Reagan had been in office for two years. Paul Volcker had been chairman of the Federal Reserve Board for nearly three. The tax-cutting policies of Reagan and the inflation-fighting policies of Volcker were beginning to take hold, just as corporate America was coming to grips with its own rather serious problems.

The fortuitous confluence of lower taxes and falling inflation and interest rates, coupled with renewed corporate efficiency, spawned a roaring bull market that would rival the wild ride that Wall Street rode in the 1920s.

Between August 1982 and January 1987, the Dow Industrials shot up over 1000 points, more than doubling the Dow's value. The gains, strong, steady, and persistent, emboldened stock traders to take more and more risks as the ugly memories of the 1970s and early 1980s slowly began to fade.

The 1980s were heady days on Wall Street, even if Main Street failed to notice until late in the decade of greed. Stock and bond traders found new respectability and rebuilt lost fortunes. Takeover artists and corporate raiders made millions through mergers and acquisitions. Names like Icahn, Jacobs, Pickens, and Steinberg sent chills up the spines of entrenched corporate managers. Men like Milken, Boesky, Siegel, and Levine embodied all that was both revered and reviled on Wall Street in the Roaring Eighties.

But the great bull market of the 1980s was also largely a professional affair in which the public failed to participate. Mutual funds and day traders were scarcely factors in the bull market of the 1980s. (Ironically, that may be the reason the 1980s were labeled the Decade of Greed. No such appellation is accorded the bull run

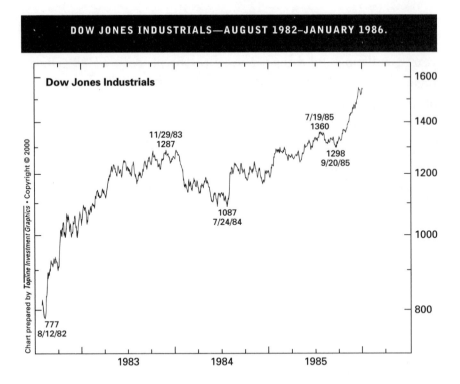

DOW JONES INDUSTRIALS—AUGUST 1982–JANUARY 1986.

Dow Jones Industrials

11/29/83
1287

7/19/85
1360

1298
9/20/85

1087
7/24/84

777
8/12/82

Chart prepared by *Topline Investment Graphics* • Copyright © 2000

of the 1990s, the decade in which stock prices have outperformed
the 1980s by a wide margin. The enrichment of Main Street, as well
as Wall Street, seems to have gone a long way in ameliorating the
class envy that was so evident over a decade ago.)

But as the rich got enormously wealthy in the market run, by
early 1987 there were growing signs that the stock market was
becoming increasingly unstable. Volatility in the market was
becoming unusually vicious. With the Dow at 1700, it was becoming increasingly common for the bellwether average to move in a
50-to-100-point range in a single day. (Remember, these are the
1980s we're talking about. At 1700, a 50-point move was worth
nearly 3 percent. In 1999, when the Dow was at 10,000, a 3 percent move, worth 300 points, got everyone's attention!)

The volatility was enhanced by computerized program trading
that allowed traders to funnel huge sums of money in and out of
the stock market with the push of a button. By January of 1987,

program trading was causing large gyrations in stock prices, helping to set the stage for greater volatility yet to come.

As the stock market moved inexorably higher that year, the underlying fundamental and technical aspects of the market and economy were deteriorating quite quickly.

The twin budget and trade deficits were seemingly spiraling out of control. They would both hit record highs just as the Dow topped out at over 2700 in August. The dollar, pressured by a variety of factors, was plunging in value against the Japanese yen, German mark, and British pound. The dollar's weakness raised fears that foreign investors, stung by the currency's sudden loss of value, would dump their U.S. stocks and bonds, pressuring both markets dramatically. Trade tensions between the United States and Germany were running high while military tensions between the United States and Iran were also escalating.

But even as those fundamental factors were building, the Dow moved higher and higher.

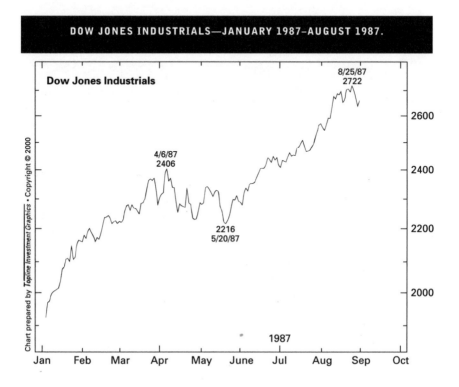

DOW JONES INDUSTRIALS—JANUARY 1987–AUGUST 1987.

Throughout the first half of the year, the Dow put on quite a show. In only eight months, the Dow vaulted from 1700 to 2722.42, hitting that peak on August 25. It was a remarkable move that had capped off five years of steady and spectacular gains for the stock market.

But from the start of the year, there were plenty of signs that the good times wouldn't last. Several markets and a variety of different indicators flashed warning signals that the stock market was indeed unstable.

The first warning sign came very early in the year. The Dow Jones Utility Average, a collection of electric utility and natural gas company stocks, peaked in January 1987. Utility stocks, because of their heavy borrowing costs, are highly sensitive to changes in interest rates. (We will illustrate that in greater detail later in the book.) Since utility stocks serve as a stock market proxy for interest rates, their behavior is closely watched for clues as to what the future direction of rates will be.

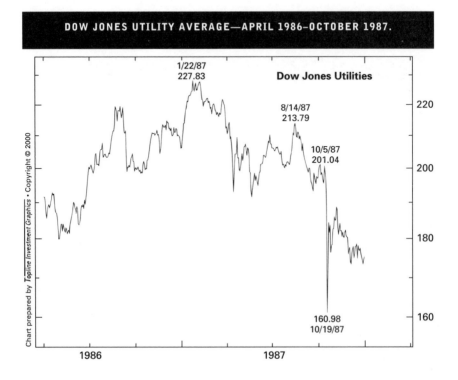

DOW JONES UTILITY AVERAGE—APRIL 1986–OCTOBER 1987.

The Utility Average had been rallying sharply in previous months as interest rates continued an impressive decline begun in early 1980. But suddenly, and without warning, utility stocks started falling in January 1987 and suffered a serious decline for the next 10 months. It was a bad omen for the stock market and for interest rates.

By April 1987, Treasury bond yields fell below 7 percent and then rose more quickly and more steeply than they had in decades.

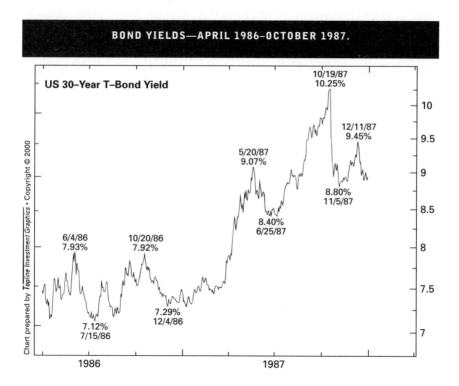

The shocking rise in interest rates, from under 7 percent to nearly 10 percent, would be one of the most serious contributing factors in the crash of 1987. The rise in rates was foretold 4 months earlier by the decline in the interest rate–sensitive Utility Average. It was a warning that went totally unheeded.

Another serious message was being sent to stock market investors, one that had been flashing for an even longer period of time. A key technical indicator that can be helpful in predicting the long-term direction of stocks, the so-called advance/decline line, had broken down completely. It had peaked out months before the crash but was ignored by the majority of traders and investors.

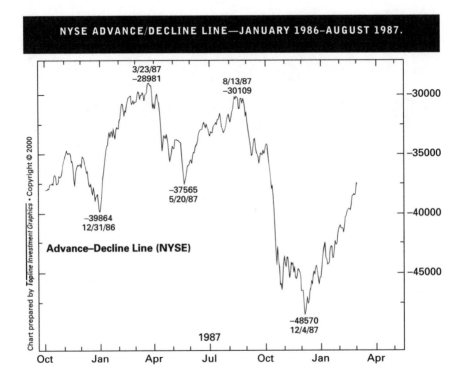

NYSE ADVANCE/DECLINE LINE—JANUARY 1986–AUGUST 1987.

The advance/decline (A/D) line is a measure of the stock market's underlying momentum. Technical analysts, who use charts to predict the future direction of the market, keep very close tabs on the A/D line. Simply put, the advance/decline line shows how many New York Stock Exchange stocks are going up in value every day compared to how many are going down. The more stocks going up every day, the healthier the overall stock market appears to be. The more stocks going down, the weaker the market's underlying health. Chart watchers take the net number of advances or declines every day (declines subtracted from advances) and plot it on a graph. That's how the daily advance/decline line is built.

The most dangerous condition that occurs in the stock market can occur when popular averages like the Dow or the S&P 500 are making new highs, while the advance/decline line proceeds to new lows.

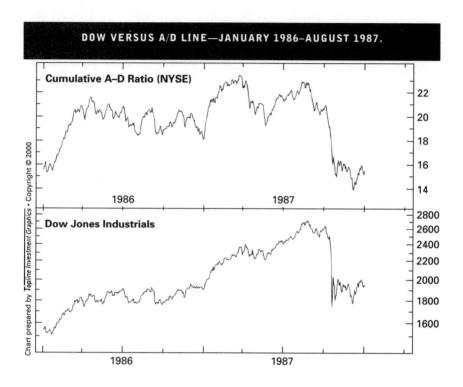

As the chart clearly illustrates, the market was uneven from mid-1986 through the summer of 1987. While the Dow went on to a series of new highs, the majority of stocks traded on the New York Stock Exchange fell, day after day after day. Market technicians call this a *negative divergence*. It is a potent message that investors needed to respect, but didn't. Indeed, the stock market was sending out a message about itself. The message was an attempt to warn investors that the overall stock market was unhealthy and unstable, despite the remarkable performances by some popular stock market averages.

(A similar negative divergence became increasingly evident in late 1999 and early 2000, when the advance/decline line plunged to a series of new lows as the Dow jumped above 11,700. It had been in a steady decline for nearly two years. How it played out at the time of this writing was still an unsolved market puzzle.)

But while that divergence was discussed almost daily in the financial press and on financial television, most investors were caught completely flat-footed in the October deluge. I should also hasten to note that not all such divergences lead to complete calamity in the stock market. There have been numerous times when the Dow has gone to new highs while the advance/decline line moved to new lows and then recovered, broadening the scope of the market's rally. But there have been only three times in the second half of this century when the divergence was as pronounced as it was in the summer of 1987. The first occurred in 1973 and 1974, the second in 1987, and the third from April 1998 to February 2000. In two of those cases, the subsequent damage to the market was quite severe.

The warnings did not stop there. The Dow Transportation Average, an index of plane, train, and truck stocks, also sent a massive sell signal to investors several days before the crash.

Chart watchers on Wall Street have a theory that suggests the Dow Jones Industrial Average and the Dow Jones Transportation Average should move in tandem. Their reasoning is quite plain. Assume that the Dow Jones Industrial Average, a group of 30 industrial companies, represents the manufacturing prowess of the U.S. economy. The Transports, whose companies ship manufactured goods and travelers all over the country, represent the vigor of the economy. More simply, the Industrials tell us how strong, or weak, production is. The Transports tell us how strong or weak demand is throughout the economy. In the best of all worlds, the Industrials and Transports should travel to new highs together, reflecting strong production and strong demand. If the Industrials rally without the Transports, then manufacturers are producing more goods than are desired by consumers. That could lead to a buildup of unsaleable inventories and, ultimately, recession.

This method of tracking the Dow Industrials and the Dow Transports is known as the *Dow Theory*. It is the oldest form of technical analysis employed on Wall Street.

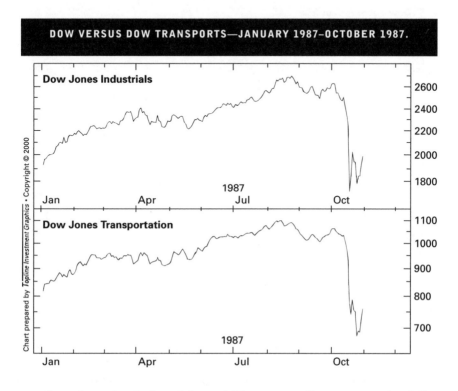

DOW VERSUS DOW TRANSPORTS—JANUARY 1987–OCTOBER 1987.

So, when the Industrials and Transports diverge meaningfully, as they did in the autumn of 1987, a recession signal was sent. Consequently, the Dow Theory generated an important sell signal for the stock market. On Thursday, October 15, 1987, the red light flashed. Had investors listened to that message, they could have escaped the ravages of the following Monday and saved themselves the most painful experience in modern market history.

The most eerie message of the stock market in 1987 came from the trading pattern the market was tracing out since the beginning of the year. Some very savvy market watcher noticed in the summer of 1987 that the Dow Industrial Average, throughout 1987, was repeating the exact pattern established in 1929.

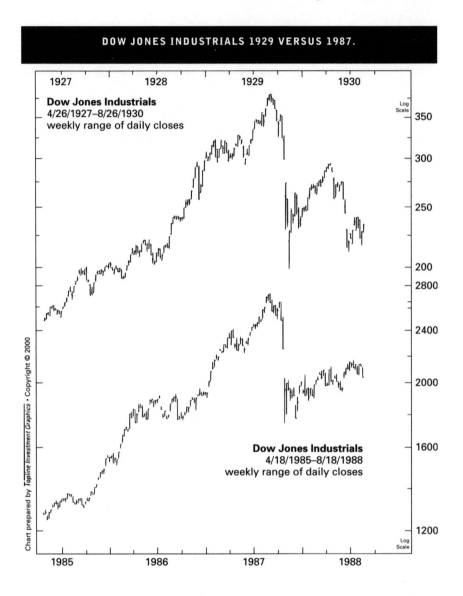

DOW JONES INDUSTRIALS 1929 VERSUS 1987.

Dow Jones Industrials
4/26/1927–8/26/1930
weekly range of daily closes

Log Scale

Dow Jones Industrials
4/18/1985–8/18/1988
weekly range of daily closes

Chart prepared by *Topline Investment Graphics* • Copyright © 2000

The similarities were frightening to chart watchers on Wall Street. The Dow Jones Industrial Average was moving, day by day, in lockstep with a pattern traced out nearly 60 years before. If one used a lunar calendar (where months are 28 days long) the Dow both peaked and crashed on the exact same day in both years.

The market was sending a message about *itself* that only a few investors took to heart. One such trader, whose story I chronicled in a previous book, *Traders' Tales,* made $13 million betting that the trading pattern in 1987 would resolve itself in exactly the same manner it had in 1929! Now that's a great example of listening to the message of the market.

The warning signs, however, were not confined to the stock market. The most potent message came from the bond market, the stock market's alter ego. The bond market is the market in which interest rates are determined. As interest rates fall, stock prices tend to rise. Low interest rates make it easy for businesses to borrow and expand, for consumers to borrow and buy, and for investors to borrow and trade. The opposite is true of rising interest rates.

In the spring of 1987, interest rates suddenly stopped falling, just as the Dow Utility Average correctly forecast would happen in January of that year. From April 1987 forward, long-term interest rates, for a variety of reasons, would spike from just about 7 percent to nearly 10 percent in the space of only six short months. Rising rates reduce the value of stocks dramatically. If investors suddenly realize they can make 7, 8, 9, or even 10 percent by investing in risk-free bonds instead of more risky stocks, they will quickly shift their funds from stocks to bonds, depressing stock prices in the process.

The speed with which interest rates rose in the middle of 1987 should have alerted investors that something in the economic outlook was changing. It didn't. Interest rates would not fall again until the week of the crash.

Finally, the plunging value of the dollar was a message that should have been heard around the world in that fateful year. The U.S. dollar was the world's most troubled currency in 1987, free-falling as the U.S. economy began to wobble under a mountain of debt. The federal budget deficit was setting new records on a monthly basis. The U.S. merchandise trade deficit grew just as quickly. Insatiable American consumers bought billions of dollars worth of imported goods, while American exporters struggled to sell their goods overseas. To rectify the yawning trade gap, Reagan Administration officials, in 1985, sought to weaken the dollar in an effort to boost American exports to the rest of the world. All other things being equal, a weaker dollar makes American goods less expensive overseas, boosting exports. But a precipitous decline in the dollar's value had not helped America's trade balance between 1985 and 1987. Indeed, the trade deficit exploded to a new record of $17 billion in August of 1987 (reported by the government in October of that year). Anxious currency traders sold the dollar with reckless abandon as the trade deficit grew and grew, pushing it into a near free fall. The collapse of the dollar, while necessary to redress those growing trade imbalances, created other problems in the fall of 1987.

Foreign investors who had so eagerly purchased U.S. stocks and bonds in the great bull market of the 1980s found that their investments, while rising in dollar terms, were falling in value after they converted their dollars back into pounds, yen, or German marks. They rushed to sell their stock and bond holdings in 1987, helping to precipitate the October crash.

A country's currency holds only as much value as investors are willing to accord it, on a relative basis. If a country has a strong economy, sound fiscal and monetary policies, budget surpluses and trade surpluses, then investors can do only one thing—buy the currency so that they can invest in that healthy country. The United States in 1987 had none of the above. The dollar was sending a potent message that the U.S. economy was on perilous ground. The dollar's message was unequivocal. The U.S. government desperately needed to address its problems without delay.

But by the time most investors bothered to pay attention to the dollar's warning, it was too late.

On October 19, 1987, the Dow Jones Industrial Average plunged from roughly 2240 to 1732 by day's end. Many investors had ignored all the previous messages being sent by a number of markets. They would get one more quite potent message that very day.

In the short trading day, a half-trillion dollars in stock market value would be vaporized, leaving traders and investors shell-shocked on exchange floors all over the country. (Today, a 22.7 percent decline in NYSE stocks alone would wipe out about $3 trillion in market value.)

Curiously, the message of the crash was confined only to Wall Street and Washington. Unlike the Crash of 1929, this stock market debacle would not usher in a new depression. In fact, the U.S. economy continued to grow in 1988 and 1989. It grew briskly. Corporate profits hit record levels in the year after the crash and the recession that many observers predicted (myself included) simply never materialized.

Main Street may never know how close it came, however, to experiencing anew the agony of the 1920s. Only the quick thinking of Federal Reserve Chairman Alan Greenspan and his counterparts in the Reagan Administration kept the crash from spilling over from Wall Street to Main Street. The Fed flushed billions of dollars into the economy, slashing interest rates, and helping to arrange the rescue of troubled financial firms. (The Fed would respond similarly and appropriately to several financial crises that gripped the world in the 1990s as well.)

But on Wall Street, the 1987 crash did bring hard times. Some 35,000 traders and brokers lost their jobs in subsequent years. Many trading firms and a few brokerage houses went out of business or were merged into bigger, healthier Wall Street establishments.

Reforms came to the New York Stock Exchange. New limits were placed on computerized program trading. Other risky stock market strategies were curtailed in the aftermath of the crash.

Regulators designed two new rules to make the financial markets safer and more efficient than they had been before.

The crash did not deliver a message without meaning. The crash of 1987 meant unemployment for tens of thousands of Wall Street professionals. It signaled the end of a decade-long rise in real estate values both in New York City and, to an extent, in the high flying Southern California property market.

But for many people on Main Street, the message of the crash may have fallen on deaf ears. The net effect on the individual American, or even the individual investor, was nil. Many Americans were taught by the relatively rapid recovery on Wall Street that one should always "buy the dip" when stock prices decline. While that strategy has worked uncharacteristically well in the 13 years after the crash, there may be a time when buying stocks after a severe decline is, very simply, the wrong thing to do.

We'll only know, as a late colleague of mine used to say, "in the fullness of time."

2

Practical Magic

You're probably thinking, at this point, those were interesting stories, but what do they have to do with me?

It's a good question. If you had watched the market's behavior on November 22, 1963, there scarcely would have been a way for you to avoid the brutal sell-off that was triggered by JFK's assassination. Nor was it likely that, had you been there, you would have paid heed to the stock market's message in October 1929. Only a few savvy investors did. But those few savvy investors managed to save themselves from the economic nightmare just ahead.

But that is exactly the point of this book. What if you did pay attention to what the market says, not just what it does? Would you be better off? Would your investments be better protected? Would you make better-timed, big-ticket purchases or even save some money on gasoline or heating oil or food? It's quite possible.

In the following sections, we will explore how the stock market and the real economy interrelate. How does Wall Street's behavior give us an early look at Main Street's future? How can the stock market tell you which sectors of the economy are hot and which are not? How can the price movement of an individual stock help you make a better, more informed decision about your career?

Believe it or not, both the absolute and relative movement of stock prices have the power to do just that. Companies and industries that appear to have bright futures ahead of them usually have rising stock prices. Look at the behavior of technology stocks from the late 1970s to the present day. Clearly not every technology company that had a soaring stock price in the early 1980s is a market leader today. But, on balance, technology stocks have been the big winners of the last two decades.

Similarly, the old engines of the American economy, auto companies, steel companies, and the like, have not enjoyed the same momentum on Wall Street as they once did. As Bethlehem Steel's importance to the U.S. economy waned, its share price declined accordingly. Plot a graph of Bethlehem Steel against IBM, or more recently America Online, and look at the differences. Their prices speak volumes about both the past and the future.

In this section, we explore how to pick up practical tips from the market's many messages and how to rethink what Wall Street means to you. Wall Street, as much as being a place, is also a state of mind. And that subtle shift in perception can make a not-so-subtle difference to you.

As you move through these stories, you will no doubt want to know how you can apply these messages to your own life and chosen livelihood. At CNBC.com, a series of web pages has been established to help you make better use of the contents of this book.

In our Message of the Markets web pages, CNBC has provided a stock charting service (as does Dow Jones Interactive) that will allow you to draw stock charts of the company for which you work. You can compare your company's stock activity to other companies in your industry, in other industries, and against certain stock market indexes as well. Such tools allow you to see where your firm stands versus its peers and versus other leading companies.

By accessing Hoover's business information service, through CNBC.com, you can add to your knowledge of your company's financial status. Hoover's provides in-depth information and analysis of all publicly traded companies.

Boom and Bust

The financial markets have always played an integral role in anticipating the business cycle. Historically, stocks, bonds, and commodities have behaved in certain, predictable ways at both the
beginning and the end of an economic recovery. The business cycle
itself also has behaved predictably in many of America's previous
economic cycles.

It is that very predictability that has allowed financial markets to
fully anticipate and, more important, signal the seismic shifts that
often take place at the beginning and the end of both boom and bust.

Before we examine how the markets send signals about the business cycle, it would make sense to look at the business cycle itself.

As expressed by modern economists, the business cycle runs a
fairly standard course. The first stage is one of expansion, or recovery. On average, expansions or recoveries have lasted roughly
between four and six years in this century. Recessions, excluding the
Great Depression, are generally far shorter in length, averaging
roughly one to two years. Appropriately, bear markets are shorter
than bull markets, as well. (The 1930s and 1970s were exceptions
to the general rule. The 1930s, while dotted with some sporadic
economic upturns, was generally a decade of recession. The 1970s,
meanwhile, had both rapid accelerations and sharp retrenchments
throughout that volatile period. The financial markets, despite the
unusual nature of both periods, moved appropriately in advance of
both conditions.) As for the generic cycle, when recessions reach
their nadir, the process begins anew and the recovery takes hold.

In very general terms, a recession usually brings about declining
interest rates, which fall as the economic slowdown convinces bond
market investors that inflation, the bane of the bond market's existence, will disappear as the economy slows down. Bonds anticipate
the slowdown or recession by rallying. As bonds go up in price,
their yields fall, reflecting those declining inflation expectations.

The stock market, taking its cue from falling interest rates,
begins to rally, in some cases almost inexplicably, since most

investors or average citizens fail to recognize the stimulative effect of falling rates.

Finally, commodity prices begin to rise as the economy strengthens and the demand for goods and services heats up. It is that renewed demand that allows both companies and individuals to pay rising prices for "stuff." The process continues until policymakers perceive rising prices as a threat to the economic expansion. The inflation scare prompts policymakers, in America's case, the Federal Reserve, to raise interest rates. The rate hikes eventually slow the economy, or cause a recession if the Fed has to move aggressively to rein in inflation.

And so the cycle begins again.

The still infamous Karl Marx was among the first economists to recognize the inherent boom and bust tendencies of capitalist economies. Marx believed the intense cyclicality of market capitalism would eventually lead to its downfall. He was wrong. Nikolai Kondratieff, a Lenin-era economist hired by the Bolsheviks to prove Marx right, studied business cycles in the West in the early 1900s. Using price data on commodities like wheat and corn, dating back to seventeenth-century England, Kondratieff found that capitalist economies moved in waves. There were short waves in which cyclical recessions and recoveries alternated with great regularity. He also discovered long waves of general prosperity and massive busts that followed, roughly every 60 years.

In a sense, he proved Marx correct. Capitalist economies did tend to swing regularly from recovery to recession or from boom to bust. But much to the displeasure of the Russian government, he also observed that in each recession, the seeds of recovery were sewn. That was true both for regular recessions and recoveries and for the longer waves that crested in the West. Unfortunately for Kondratieff, his inability to prove that capitalism would soon crash under the weight of its own bourgeois excesses earned him a trip to prison, rather than a Nobel Prize in economics.

What neither Kondratieff nor Marx knew was that the markets themselves contained the information that foretold the coming of capitalism's strongest and weakest points of those cycles.

Of course, many modern Western economists also fail to use the financial markets as forecasting tools that could help them to anticipate the big and meaningful turns in the economy that are so important to everyone.

In a "normal" economic expansion, the first signs of recovery can be seen in the stock and bond markets. In one of the most obvious examples in recent memory, the Dow Jones Industrial Average began an explosive bull market move on August 17, 1982, that would accurately foretell one of the greatest economic expansions in modern times.

After a series of punishing blows to the U.S. economy in the late 1970s and early 1980s, no one on Wall Street or on Main Street was ready to hear the siren song of the stock market in the summer of 1982. Economists frequently predicted yet another dismal year for the U.S. economy as the nation suffered through its deepest and most severe recession since the 1930s.

We all remember its chief characteristics. Surging inflation, rising interest rates, and double-digit unemployment had become the norm between 1980 and 1982. At the start of the decade, banks would raise their prime lending rate to 20.5 percent. Inflation peaked at 13 percent as did the nation's unemployment rate. After the twin oil shocks of the 1970s, the humiliating Iranian hostage crisis, and a deepening sense of "malaise," very few Americans could believe that a renaissance was about to arrive. Only the markets knew what was to come, even as the prophets of doom proclaimed the dark days would last forever. Wall Street veterans recall a now infamous *Business Week* cover story in 1982, declaring "The Death of Equities." Ironically, that dire prediction would mark the stock market's low point, from which it has still not returned.

The stock market "broke out" in August 1982, staging impressive rallies in the late summer as volume at the New York Stock Exchange exploded almost inexplicably.

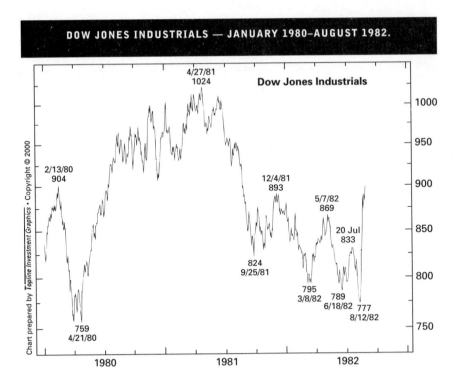

DOW JONES INDUSTRIALS — JANUARY 1980–AUGUST 1982.

For two years, the Dow had been suffering a vicious bear market, torn about by the economic conditions that simultaneously ravaged Wall Street. After crossing 1000 for the first time in 1966, the Dow would not recapture that ground in a meaningful way for 16 years. By August 1982, the blue chip average would rest at 777, the lowest level it had seen in at least five years and fully 25 percent below the millennial mark that had been first touched when Lyndon Johnson was president.

Even as stocks plunged back to their lows, something very important was taking place. Bond market interest rates stopped rising and bond prices stopped falling. The interest rate decline began as investors and consumers were still betting that inflation and unemployment would rise together forever. Individual investors scrambled to purchase bank certificates of deposit (CDs) that were yielding 13 percent or so. They should have been buying stocks and bonds. The bond market was sending an important message about the future. Few people heard the call.

The bond market's rally had its roots in a disaster that few saw coming. But it was an event that would help bring about recovery here in the United States. Something very curious happened in that hot and difficult summer. Another economic disaster was brewing.

Latin American nations, to whom many of America's biggest banks had lent billions of dollars, were on the ropes economically. On top of America's other big problems, Latin American debtors, particularly Mexico, threatened to default on their debt payments to large American banks like Citicorp (now Citigroup) and Chase Manhattan.

The debt crisis brought Wall Street's troubles to a booming crescendo. There was a danger that America's biggest and once proudest financial institutions were about to crumble under the weight of Latin American debt. Too preoccupied with their own problems, few on Main Street were even aware of the budding crisis that threatened to turn a terrible recession into another great depression.

But Federal Reserve Chairman Paul Volcker rang the bell that signaled the start of a new bull market. Promising to bail out the nation's big banks in the event of a Mexican debt default, Volcker rapidly provided ample liquidity to keep the banks from collapsing. The Federal Reserve rapidly expanded the nation's money supply, while slashing interest rates dramatically. The dramatic drop in rates sent the stock market soaring. Bond market interest rates plunged from historically high levels in 1980, when the bellwether 30-year bond yield hit 14 percent, all the way down to 6 percent in 1986.

But even as Paul Volcker was making it clear that he would slash rates to rejuvenate the economy, most people believed the new crisis to be a new beginning for more troubled times. The markets interpreted the events quite differently.

Wall Street veterans have an expression that mirrors the notion that it's always darkest before the dawn. The veterans say "bailouts are bullish." The stock market clearly held that view in 1986. Economist Jason Trennert of the ISI Group, a New York economic consulting firm, notes that crises are good for financial assets because they generally lead to lower interest rates.

Indeed, as the Fed rushed to bail out the banks, the rush of liquidity (the explosion of new money created by the Fed) fueled a rapid rise in the stock market and drove interest rates sharply lower. Those market events, which no one believed would last at the time, created an environment in which the economy could flourish. Businesses could borrow more cheaply. Companies could sell stock to raise funds more successfully. Consumers, freed from the shackles of punitive lending rates, bought homes, cars, and furniture.

Businesses expanded as pent-up consumer demand exploded. (Some fairly aggressive tax cuts and even more aggressive government spending plans in the early 1980s helped to get the boom going as well.)

But it was the markets that first recognized what was about to happen. The Dow began a five-year bull run that would take the blue chips from 777 in August of 1982 to 2722 in August 1987.

On Wall Street, a bell is metaphorically rung before major events occur. In 1982, the bell sounded loud and clear. The only problem was, as always, only a few smart people heard it ringing. It is vital to recognize the important nature of market signals like these. When several markets are in lockstep, either up or down, the forecasting power can be quite remarkable. In the main, falling interest rates, rising stock prices, gently rising commodity prices, and a stable currency can signal that an economy, any economy, is on the verge of a period of sustained noninflationary growth. Those signals are the most potent and oftentimes allow investors to make significant sums with a big bet on the "big picture."

NOTE: Our Message of the Markets page at CNBC.com provides a host of economic indicators for your perusal. From the current signals being flashed by important stock market averages to key interest rate and commodity indicators, the Message of the Markets web pages will help you make informed personal forecasts of where the overall economy is headed.

Stocks and Jobs

One of the most fascinating things about the stock market is not just that it can help you see where the overall economy is going but, at times, it can even help you see where *you* are going in the overall economy.

Let me explain.

Every day investors make bets, informed bets to be sure, but bets on which industries and companies are likely to succeed in the future. That's what investors get paid to do. Real investors, from venture capitalists to mutual fund managers, are in the business of finding businesses that will grow and prosper. The prospects for that growth and prosperity are reflected in the stock prices of the companies with the greatest growth and profit potential.

It makes sense, then, for everyone to use the stock market as a barometer of his or her own company's, and its industry's, health.

Let's say, for instance, you work in the computer field. The stock of your company, ABC Computing, is rising. The shares of your company's competitors are also rising. In fact, technology stocks of all stripes are going up and appear to be in a secular bull market that will continue for some time. It seems safe to say that you are working for a company in an industry that is dynamic, growing, and flush with opportunities.

But what if ABC Computing's stock is going down while all the others are going up? What if ABC Computing is going up while all other computer stocks are going down? What if ABC Computing and all other computer stocks are falling simultaneously? The market might be trying to tell you something. And you should listen.

While investors sometimes make mistakes by getting either too enthusiastic or too disdainful about a company or an industry's future, Wall Street's longer-term judgments are sound. There is plenty of market history to prove that. If you need to see it for yourself, just examine how the stock market has changed over time, always reflecting the changing composition of the economy itself.

In 1896, when the Dow Jones Industrial Average was first tabulated, it consisted of 12 stocks. One of them, The Pullman Company, was a staple of industrial America at the turn of the century. The railcar maker was a blue chip company that provided railroad companies with the luxurious passenger cars that became synonymous with the proud firm's name. The firm is no longer one of the Dow 30; it doesn't even exist anymore. Only one of the original components of the Dow Industrials remains in the index—General Electric. (GE is the parent of CNBC.) Like the market as a whole, GE has frequently changed with the times and is now the most valuable company in the world, with a market value of roughly $540 billion.

In today's rapidly evolving global economy, the stock market is sending a clear signal about the expected winners in the information age. Internet stocks, communications technology stocks, and wireless communications stocks have been extremely big winners on Wall Street in the last several years.

Food stocks, basic industry stocks, and shares of commodity companies have been big losers. That should tell you something about how the future of the economy is likely to unfold. It is always possible, of course, that the technology revolution could fail or that a recession or depression could alter the pace and scope of economic change. Indeed, in that environment, many investors buy defensive stocks like food, drink, tobacco, and drug stocks because, even in the worst of times, people eat, drink, smoke, and treat their ills. But absent any earth-shattering disruption to progress, the U.S. stock market at the dawn of the new millennium was betting heavily that a new economic age, driven by rapid technological change, was about to begin.

In similar fashion, at the turn of the last century the stock market made enormous bets on the industrialization of America. That bet was a big winner, as the auto industry transformed the economy of the United States. Henry Ford and Alfred P. Sloan, the founders of Ford and General Motors respectively, altered forever the economic and social fabric of American life. Entirely new industries

sprang up to serve the automakers' needs. Cities flourished, the suburbs sprawled to unprecedented size, and the economy boomed.
The stock market fully anticipated the change, which was reflected
in the prices of that era's leading stocks.

While agricultural companies continued to flourish, their
importance to the overall economy eventually waned. That dimin-
ishing importance was reflected in the prices of agricultural stocks.
Indeed, only a handful of important agricultural entities trade on
the public stock market today.

As the twentieth century wore on, industrial firms began to lose
their luster. Major industrial companies saw their peak stock prices
and peak market power drop in the early 1970s. They have been
mediocre market performers, relative to their high-tech counterparts, in the last quarter of the century.

At each stage of the economy's development, the stock market
sends important messages about the prospective winners and losers
in the struggle for economic viability.

And that's the whole point of this exercise. The charts of all
these individual stocks can serve as useful barometers of their economic life expectancies. And that, in turn, can be a tool in aiding
your efforts to find gainful employment.

The Wall Street Journal Interactive Edition has a wonderful
web page that allows anyone to quickly analyze an industry and
measure how a given company is faring against its competitors and
within its sector. The Dow Jones Industry Group Center page offers
a simple and effective way to examine a company's market performance and quickly gather other pertinent financial information about
that firm. This web page can be a useful resource for you when you
are trying to decide in which industry and at which company you
would like to work.

The annals of corporate history and the history of Wall Street
are filled with examples of how the stock market *seemed* to know,
long before the employees did, of some pending news about a company's future—either good or bad.

In practical terms, the markets can help you make judgments

about the relative health of the company for which you work, the industry in which you compete, and the economy in which you live.

But in order to benefit from the markets' many insights, you must familiarize yourself with how the markets send messages. If you are an Internet entrepreneur, you should spend part of your working life examining the relative performance of Internet stocks. How are they behaving? Which are performing best and which appear to be in trouble? Is one sector of the Internet suddenly performing better than another in the stock market? Why?

These sorts of relative assessments can tell you a lot about where the industry is going and where the opportunities may be found in the future.

This applies to all industries. The stock market makes relative assumptions about the future every day. Is Liz Claiborne doing better than Ann Taylor? How is Coca-Cola doing relative to Pepsi? Many times these questions can be answered by the stock market. A quick peek at the charts of two competing companies' stocks will tell you volumes about how their futures are perceived in the marketplace.

That's true, as well, among industry groups. Which industry appears stronger, biotechnology or medical products? Are stocks for health maintenance organizations outperforming those for traditional health insurance companies? (Not anymore it seems.) These valuation assessments can help investors and employees pick and choose among opportunities for profits and growth. I know from personal experience and years of observation that the market knows when something is going right at a company and when something is going wrong, long before it is apparent to the casual observer.

My late mentor, Ed Hart, a veteran business news reporter, was quite astute in using the markets this way. He would notice that a particular savings and loan (S&L) institution was having trouble in the stock market. He would use the unexplained decline as the basis for further inquiry. Suddenly, he would find countless reasons why the stock was in the midst of a meaningful swoon. Next thing I knew, Ed had the whole story months before the news tickers carried word of the S&L's failure.

Ed knew better than most how the market worked. He made it work for him in such a way that he provided useful information for the viewers who counted on his insights. I often remarked that Ed left breadcrumbs on the road to the gingerbread house for our audience. In reality, it is the market that does that. It's everyone's job to pick the crumbs up.

In this segment of the book, we'll examine how the stock market sends important messages about different industries and which companies may be ripe for continued growth in the U.S. economy and which may not. We'll also show how the stock market has accurately forecast the declines, dénouements, and even deaths of not just individual companies but whole industries, as well.

Each graph and each story will serve as a potent reminder that the message of the markets can't be ignored—even when you're *not* investing and even if you're *only* looking for a job.

The stock market has served this function for literally hundreds of years. In the 1850s, as railroads were born, the financial markets gave birth to a brisk trade in railroad securities. Railroad bonds became the principal vehicles through which one could share in the future of this transformational industry. The construction of regional railways and, ultimately, the transcontinental railroad, revolutionized American life and business.

As Art Cashin, of PaineWebber, pointed out many times to CNBC viewers, shares of railroad companies proliferated by the turn of the twentieth century. The markets accurately identified the awesome power of this new transportation technology and accorded railroad stocks and bonds their proper premium.

That's why using the stock market to identify opportunities has become so important. The market often tells us just how important new developments can be: from the construction of the nation's rail system to the invention of the telegraph, telephone, radio, or Internet. The markets can also be quite helpful in assessing the viability of existing businesses and the opportunities they may offer, not just to individual investors, but to individual workers as well.

Radio Days

In some ways, the early days of radio may prove somewhat analogous to the development of the Internet today, at least from a Wall Street perspective. Like the Internet, radio proved to be a transformational technology that changed the communications industry forever. And like the Internet, radio stocks enjoyed the same exalted status in the 1920s that Net stocks enjoy today. And like the Internet, radio shares zoomed higher during the greatest bull market of that age.

One could, of course, argue that the invention of the telephone was more similar to the development of the Internet. The telephone wrought changes in interpersonal communications that have yet to be duplicated. In fact, only the Internet may serve to alter the communications landscape as dramatically as the telephone.

But Wall Street's fascination with the Internet echoes its fascination with radio, both in terms of the speed with which the new technology was recognized and in terms of the speculative frenzy with which investors bought and sold shares.

Consider the history of radio's most successful proponent, the Radio Corporation of America (RCA). Its stock had a storied history on Wall Street. It was one of the darlings of the Roaring Twenties bull market. RCA and its National Broadcasting Company (NBC) Radio Network were owned by General Electric back in those early days. It would be sold in later years only to be reacquired by GE in the mid-1980s. Ironically, GE would sell most of RCA's television-making operations but hang on to its NBC Television Network, bringing the peacock full circle. General Electric owns NBC and my network, CNBC, even today.

In 1923 RCA shares traded as low as $21 apiece and vaulted to $500 by 1929. Wall Street investors made huge bets on the growth of radio and they were right about its vast potential. In 1920, there were only 5000 in-home radios in use in the United States. By 1924, that figure ballooned to 2.5 million. RCA's revenue from "wireless" communications reached $4 million in 1925, while the

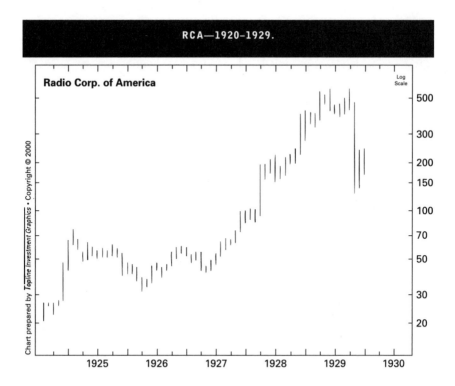

RCA—1920–1929.

Radio Corp. of America

Log Scale

500
300
200
150
100
70
50
30
20

Chart prepared by *Topline Investment Graphics* • Copyright © 2000

1925   1926   1927   1928   1929   1930

sale of radiolas, the original name for a radio receiver, generated an additional $46 million (12).

Even when Wall Street was still in its relative infancy, the stock market sent out messages as fast as any radio signal. The stock of RCA was a phenomenon in its time, as was the development of the technology from which it profited.

The growth of this transformational industry was extremely rapid, much like the growth of the Internet today. In 1920, radio station KDKA, in Pittsburgh, Pennsylvania, broadcast the results of the Harding-Cox presidential elections live. In the summer of 1921, RCA broadcast the first sporting event ever delivered to a nationwide audience: boxing's heavyweight world championship.

The rapid pace of growth continued throughout the 1920s. RCA, its parent General Electric, and another radio pioneer, Westinghouse, jointly purchased a New York radio station in 1926.

They formed the National Broadcasting Company, naming New York's WEAF the anchor station for the fledgling network. NBC quickly strung together 25 more stations. In 1927, NBC aired the Rose Bowl coast to coast. Radio was a full-fledged business.

While radio continued to grow and prosper, shares of RCA surged to their peak in 1929. The terrible Crash of 1929 and subsequent bear market would wipe out the gains from the entire six-year run.

RCA—1923–1935.

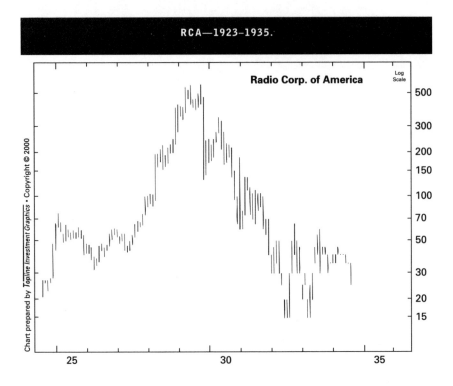

By 1935, RCA would trade down to levels not seen since 1923. It would not revisit its bull market high until the mid-1960s, when RCA's dominance of the color television industry restored its former glory.

Despite all that, radio grew in prominence as the entertainment and information medium of choice throughout the United States and the world. President Franklin D. Roosevelt cemented the medium's place in American culture with his historic fireside chats. Sporting events, radio shows, and news and weather reports became staples of American culture, all delivered by a little appliance that had been virtually unheard of only a decade before.

By its peak as the dominant communications medium in 1948, radio employed thousands of people and accounted for many millions of dollars in revenue.

It can be argued that the spectacular run-up in radio shares "priced in" all the industry's future growth. And having priced in the hereafter, radio stocks collapsed appropriately with the onset of the Great Depression.

Like RCA, the Standard & Poor's Radio Index rose and fell sharply in the 1920s and 1930s. But the message of the market in radio's early days was clear: A transformational industry was in its embryonic stages and it would change the communications landscape forever. Wall Street tuned in, long before radio's first big signals were broadcast.

The stock market, however, is not just adept at identifying new opportunities in business, it also tells investors when the relative importance of a particular industry is on the wane.

At the turn of the last century, several now defunct or irrelevant industries were represented in the Dow Jones Industrial Average. The Pullman Railcar Company was in the Dow in the early 1900s, so was Anaconda Copper. The market, eventually, recognized their declining importance and neither is remembered today. They have been replaced by more vibrant components that offer better investment and employment opportunities.

That's the market's job—to identify winners and losers in the business world and to accord their securities their appropriate relative values.

Only a few industries were ever deemed to be of supreme importance to the U.S. economy. One, of course, was the auto industry. The hundreds of auto companies that existed in the early 1900s provided fantastic opportunities to millions of Americans who worked on the assembly lines or invested in their stocks. Consumers benefited as well, gaining access to a new mode of transportation that forever altered the American landscape.

The other treasured industry was steel. While the auto business remains a key engine of economic vibrancy, steel has fallen on hard times. Once the undergirding of America's industrial strength, steel's support for the economy has softened considerably in the last three decades. In today's virtual economy, it is difficult to remember just how important steel once was. It both provided and represented the infrastructure of the U.S. economy. Countless American steel towns thrived in the era of "big steel." They corroded into recession and, in some cases, oblivion when the domestic steel industry was smelted by cheap foreign rivals.

The stock market told that tale long before big steel's decline was a foregone conclusion.

Steel Trap

Back when America was synonymous with industrial power, the steel industry stood as a symbol of the nation's manufacturing might. Steel was used in everything from skyscrapers to highway construction to auto assembly. Its importance as a vital commodity in the middle of this century was hard to overstate.

Entire local economies owed their very existence to the production of steel. Pittsburgh, Pennsylvania, and Buffalo and Lackawanna, New York, were three once thriving cities that prospered with the growing output of I-beams, flat-rolled steel, and cold-rolled sheet.

Far away from those blue-collar communities, steel also supported some white-collar workers on Wall Street. The stocks of steel companies were once as solid as the commodity they produced. That tensile strength was reflected in the price of steel stocks. But, as Wall Street once again showed, the prices of steel stocks would reflect a permanent deterioration in that tensile strength, decades before the rest of the world realized that the steel industry had reached the peak of its power in the American economy.

U.S. Steel, Bethlehem Steel, LTV Corporation, and Wheeling-Pittsburgh were among some of the best known names of the industrial era. Shares of the big steel companies were equally well known.

The steel stocks enjoyed solid gains for much of the mid-twentieth century, rising high on the back of a booming economy. In the 1940s, manufacturing accounted for better than 40 percent of America's economic output. Much of that output was supported by steel.

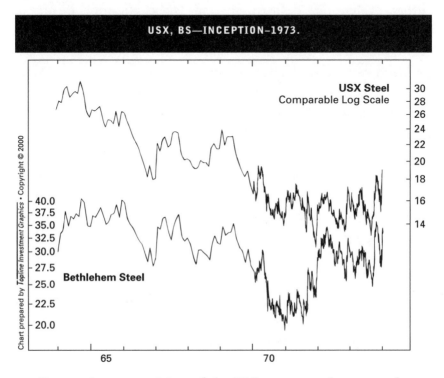

But as the composition of the U.S. economy began to change quite dramatically in the 1970s, something strange happened to the steel stocks and steel towns that had grown up around the mills. They stopped growing. Multiple recessions in the 1970s and inexpensive steel made by foreign firms ravaged the once mighty U.S. steel industry. The steel belt corroded into the rust belt as the companies, their employees, and their hometowns fell on hard times.

Employment in the steel industry fell from a record high of 726,000 jobs in 1953 to about 222,000 by 1999. Steel stocks buckled, rebounding irregularly in subsequent years. In 1979 Bethlehem Steel hit its modern peak. But employment in the industry was still declining as steel lost its preeminent place in the rapidly emerging high-tech economy. Cheap imported products that undercut high-cost American producers hastened the decline. The industry and its job base never recovered.

The stock market anticipated those cataclysmic changes and even supported key notions in the process—Joseph Schumpeter's theory of "creative destruction" and David Ricardo's theory of "competitive advantage." Schumpeter described how capitalism reinvigorates itself by tearing down inefficient industries and replacing them with more efficient competitors, while Ricardo postulated that companies that can do things more cheaply will ultimately win out over higher cost competitors. The stock market is like an economics lab where these theories are tested and proven every day.

And while domestic steel output did manage to set records late in the century when new, low-cost, highly efficient minimills reinvigorated the industry, steel employment never returned to peak levels and the importance of the steel industry to the overall economy never again approached its glory years.

A study of steel stocks shows how Wall Street fully anticipated steel's declining importance at the dawn of the information age. Stocks like Bethlehem Steel hit their peaks in the late 1970s and have been on a steady decline, even to this day. The decline is a potent reminder that Wall Street places a premium on growth, something the steel industry has not provided investors with for nearly three decades.

What does all this have to do with you, you might be wondering? The growth trajectory illustrates how market behavior can help an individual evaluate the future of a prospective employer, long before the firm's growth potential or the lack thereof becomes readily apparent to the naked eye.

For argument's sake, let's assume an individual would like a job in the steel industry today. How could he or she use the market to help pick a company with a bright future in a decaying industry?

Let's compare notes on a few companies in the field. We've already seen how Bethlehem Steel has fared in the stock market over

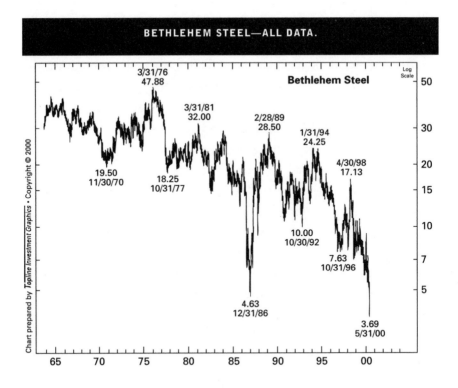

BETHLEHEM STEEL—ALL DATA.

Chart prepared by *Topline Investment Graphics* · Copyright © 2000

Bethlehem Steel

Log Scale

3/31/76
47.88

3/31/81
32.00

2/28/89
28.50

1/31/94
24.25

4/30/98
17.13

19.50
11/30/70

18.25
10/31/77

10.00
10/30/92

7.63
10/31/96

4.63
12/31/86

3.69
5/31/00

the last several decades. While the steel industry is not what it used to be, there are some companies both here and abroad that are doing quite well, turning out all kinds of steel. Nucor, one of the most highly efficient steel producers in the United States, has far outperformed Bethlehem Steel in the stock market over the last five years. Indeed, Nucor's performance in the stock market has been better than that of the steel industry as a whole. Not coincidentally, Nucor has grown more quickly and created more jobs that Bethlehem and is believed to be one of the best-run steel companies in America today.

Also not a coincidence is the relative stock market superiority of foreign firms like Mexico's Tubos de Acero or South Korea's Pohang Iron and Steel. Both have become extremely low-cost producers of steel and iron products. (They have vast pools of inexpensive labor that greatly enhance their price competitiveness.) Prospective job hunters, however, may favor Nucor, where they would likely draw a higher wage than they would overseas.

In any case, it is becoming more and more apparent how the behavior of individual stocks, relative to their peers and to their industry group as a whole, can tell you a great deal about the prospects with just the click of a computer mouse.

An even more compelling portrait of the old versus new economy can also be painted with stock charts. For a college kid trying to decide how to find gainful employment, the markets send all kinds of useful messages that, again, require just a glance.

Let's stick with Bethlehem Steel as the control in our employment experiment. How has Bethlehem Steel fared when compared to America Online (AOL) or the technology industry as a whole over the last five years? (Admittedly, few college students will agonize over whether to work in the steel industry or for an Internet company, but follow along for the sake of argument.)

While shares of Bethlehem Steel have hardly budged in the last five years, technology as a group has surged about 400 percent. Shares of AOL have vaulted somewhere in the neighborhood of 15,000 percent, making several employees stock market millionaires and creating jobs for more than 12,000 others. You can see how the market frequently makes relative decisions, choosing this industry over that one or this company over another. In a contrast as stark as this one, Wall Street is sending a very plain message. The steel industry will never again enjoy the importance it once did, either in absolute terms or relative to other, more dynamic industries or companies.

It is said that a picture paints a thousand words. If that's true, then stock charts are likely worth thousands upon thousands of dollars, to anyone interested in his or her own financial future.

It would be wise for you to look at a snapshot of your own company's performance on Wall Street. What does the chart look like? Are you working for an Internet company whose stock is surging? Or are you working for a cereal maker whose stock already has been milked of its value?

Even if your company is not publicly traded, you should look at

BS VERSUS AOL VERSUS TECH INDEX.

America Online Inc.
NYSE: AOL, split adjusted
Comparable Log Scale

DJ Technology Group
Dow Jones Total Market Index

Bethlehem Steel Corp.
NYSE: BS

how Wall Street values your industry. Many of your competitors have publicly traded stock. Look at those charts. How do you think your firm would compare?

I can tell you from personal experience that unless you're the chief executive officer (CEO) of a firm, Wall Street often knows more about your company than you do. That is not to denigrate your knowledge of your firm. But high-ranking corporate managers often tell their big, important shareholders more about the firm than they do their own workers. Consequently, your company's stock price reflects that information and gives you clues about the future of your employer. In many cases, your stock will tell you more about your firm than your boss ever will!

That's why it doesn't matter which industry you're in, it pays to listen to the message of the market to help guide your employment future.

As Wall Street sends messages about the future prospects of emerging and decaying industries, no message has ever been stronger than the one currently being sent about the Internet. In nearly unprecedented fashion, the stock market has embraced Internet stocks, sending them ever skyward, and minting million-aires and even billionaires at a mind-boggling pace.

Just as the market shunned dying industrial giants, investors have glommed onto the Internet craze in an effort to capitalize on "the new new thing." Clearly the market is sending a message about the transformative power of this new technology, this new medium. The action in Internet stocks has spoken volumes about the future of technology and communications in this brave new world. The market, in fact, is already well into the process of iden-tifying the wired world's winners and losers. As you try to select among the titans of a new industry, why not let the market be your guide?

The Net

Anyone contemplating a career in the high technology field today can't help but get excited about the Internet. This dynamic new field is creating paper billionaires by the dozens, millionaires by the hundreds, and jobs by the thousands. The relatively few barriers to entry, the low cost of starting a web site, and the wide open field in which to run have created entirely new business opportunities scarcely imagined just a few short years ago.

But believe it or not, Wall Street was well aware of the Internet's potential long before it captured Main Street's, or even the media's, attention.

Consider the stocks of several companies, now considered Internet infrastructure plays. The granddaddy of them all, Cisco Systems, has been rising for years, even before the media or the general public realized that Cisco was in the process of building and selling the routers and connectors that make the Internet possible. As much as any other stock, Cisco has been sending a message that the Internet is an important new business. Cisco should know—its business depends on the growth of the Net.

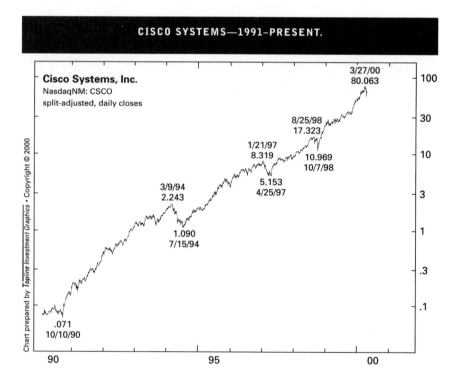

CISCO SYSTEMS—1991-PRESENT.

Even more dramatic, of course, is the explosive bull market in Net stocks themselves. The Web has captured everyone's attention and promises to be one of the important, transformational industries of all time. The creation of the Internet is said to be as important as the discovery of electricity, the invention of the telephone, the mass production of the auto, and the building of the first personal computer.

Internet devotees argue that the breadth and scope of this new business will exceed that of those just mentioned, altering dramatically and forever the way that people live, work, and play.

Venture capitalists from Silicon Valley to Silicon Alley have been making that bet for a number of years, providing capital for thousands of Internet start-ups and profiting from their emergence as publicly traded enterprises.

And while the interest in Internet stocks smacks of a mania to some observers, there is no doubt that the behavior of Internet stocks is telling us something quite important about how the U.S. and world economies will change in the coming years.

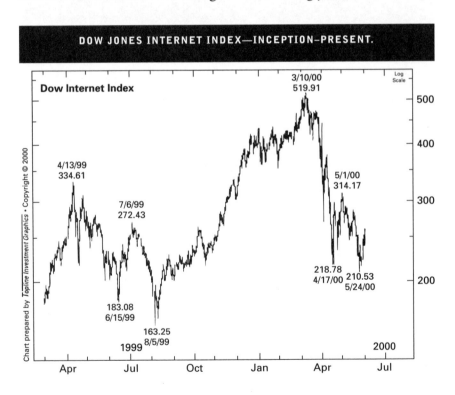

DOW JONES INTERNET INDEX—INCEPTION-PRESENT.

Let's examine a few cases in the recent past.

The first pure Internet play to hit Wall Street was Netscape. Founded by the extremely young but frighteningly intelligent Marc

Andreesen, along with Jim Clark and James Barksdale, Netscape built the first software device to help computer users navigate the World Wide Web. Netscape went public in 1995 and was an instant success in the stock market. Its opening day on Wall Street was historic as the stock spiked higher and higher, only to rally even more sharply in subsequent weeks and months.

Investors believed they had discovered something quite new. This company, it was thought, would provide the tool for both businesses and consumers to live and do business in a wholly new way, which in turn, would lead to revolutionary changes in the daily economic lives of billions of people. The stock's rally reflected the nearly infinite possibilities that the dawn of a new age promises.

Since Netscape became a publicly traded company, hundreds of other firms have followed suit. Since 1995, the industry has created tens of thousands of jobs, many of which are high paying, skilled positions that promise handsome rewards from stock options, as well.

The Dow Jones Internet Index captures graphically the incredible growth of the Internet. From its inception, only a few short years ago, the Dow Jones Composite Internet Index has quadrupled. Few embryonic industries have performed as well in their early days on Wall Street. Biotechnology enjoyed a similar status as a Wall Street darling, but the industry was more narrowly focused and, as a consequence, had fewer publicly traded companies to track its ultimate value. (We will discuss the message of the biotech market a little later in this section.)

Internet stocks have already provided fantastic stories of both rapid success and devastating failure. Jeff Bezos of Amazon.com is one of the most amazing success stories of modern business history. Starting an on-line bookstore from humble beginnings in the garage (much like Steve Jobs and Steve Wozniak at Apple Computer) of his Seattle home, Bezos built Amazon.com into a company with a market value of $30.5 billion. His own stake was worth over $10 billion when Amazon's stock hit an all-time high of $113 per share. *Time* magazine named Bezos its man of the year in 1999 for changing the way America shops.

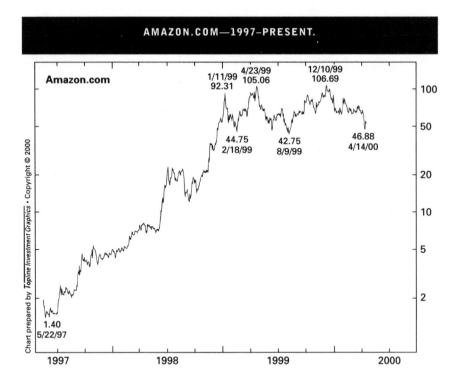

AMAZON.COM—1997–PRESENT.

Amazon has had its shares of ups and downs, as the chart clearly illustrates. At the time of this writing, the bookseller-cum-minimall had yet to turn a profit, despite explosive growth in revenues. In 1999, Amazon's sales grew to over $1.2 billion—nearly three times the level of the previous year. But losses widened to more than $400 million. The company's efforts to radically alter the retailing landscape have been amply rewarded by Wall Street in the absence of net profits.

This change to the retail landscape has been the message of the Internet revolution in both cyberspace and on Wall Street. The Net will fundamentally alter the way business is done, both between businesses and consumers and from business to business.

Indeed, in late 1999, investors began betting heavily on the success of "B-to-B" e-commerce sites. B-to-B, or business-to-business, web sites allow firms to transact business with one another, making more efficient the process of purchasing goods from suppliers, and connecting suppliers and customers more quickly and efficiently than has been done in the past. B-to-B is expected to be (pardon all the *b*'s) one of the most profitable arenas in the Internet space and may provide the most rewarding employment opportunities as well.

Oracle Corporation is a major software company whose stock benefited from the B-to-B revolution.

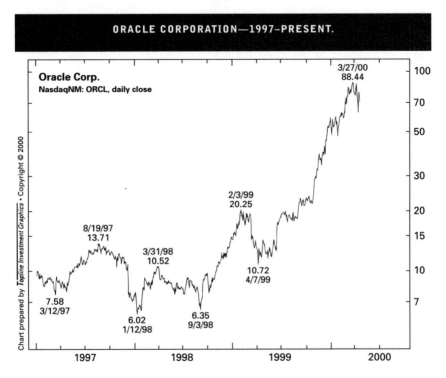

ORACLE CORPORATION—1997–PRESENT.

Led by software billionaire Larry Ellison, Oracle is in the process of helping big companies purchase their supplies over the Internet, signing a high-tech deal with Ford Motor Company in 1999. With a new site called the AutoXchange, Ford will be able to rapidly access a supply chain of thousands of companies around the world to buy the parts and services it needs to build cars. The nation's number two automaker spends at least $80 billion per year on parts, so finding a faster, more efficient way of procuring goods and services can save the company countless dollars.

Through the AutoXchange, Ford can find out in an instant which parts companies have excess windshields, for example.

Rather than wait days, weeks, or even months for their traditional windshield suppliers to deliver some badly needed glass, Ford can find a windshield maker anywhere in the world that can deliver the goods. Production delays are minimized and costs come down as Ford's assembly line keeps humming.

For this reason, many Wall Street analysts believe B-to-B e-commerce companies are good investments. The stocks of many B-to-B sites reflect that enthusiasm and are sending potent messages about the future of the Internet's development.

Wall Street catches on quickly when it comes to finding out what works in business. That prescience is often reflected in a company's stock price. The stock price then offers a hint of how a company is doing within its industry. The ebb and flow of changing perceptions is fascinating to watch. But it's the long-term trend that prospective employees should examine to determine if Wall Street likes the company for which they would like to work.

You might be wondering how a prospective employee can use this information in a helpful way as he or she searches for a job. Remember that a company's stock price is almost always sending an important message of the relative health of the underlying company. Certainly there are times when stocks go up too far, too fast. Or, they can decline sharply for no fundamental reason. But, the long-term chart of a company's stock, particularly when compared with a long-term chart of its industry, can be quite useful for getting a sense of how the company is doing relative to its peers and its industry as a whole.

Let's compare the performance of AOL to the Dow Jones Internet Index. America Online shares have rallied sharply since going public in 1992. The stock has suffered setbacks, to be sure, but it has doubled and split several times in that time frame. One thousand dollars invested in AOL in 1992 would be worth $400,000 by January 2000. The stock has been a standout in a fast-growing industry where big increases in stock values have been the norm.

America Online's revenues have grown from $3 billion in 1998 to $5 billion in 1999, a 40 percent growth rate. Its profits (yes, AOL actually earns money) have turned from sizable losses early in

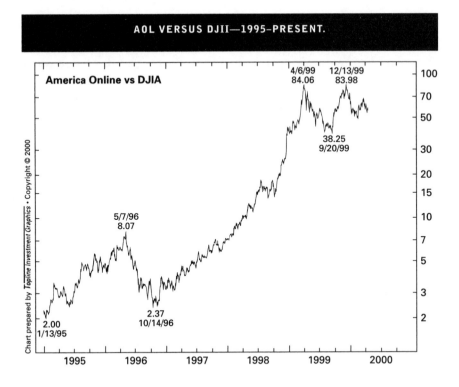

AOL VERSUS DJII—1995–PRESENT.

America Online vs DJIA

4/6/99 84.06
12/13/99 83.98
38.25 9/20/99
5/7/96 8.07
2.37 10/14/96
2.00 1/13/95

Chart prepared by *Topline Investment Graphics* · Copyright © 2000

its history into about $350 million of black ink in 1999. In its short life as a public company, AOL has created 12,100 jobs. Many employees have stock or stock options, while many more have become stock market millionaires. The company's founder, Steve Case, is worth $1.5 billion, according to *Forbes* magazine's ranking of the 400 richest Americans.

It is clear from the chart that AOL is a fast-growing company in a fast-growing industry. Maybe even more importantly, AOL also has proved that it has staying power within the industry, a bit of information that could prove quite valuable when trying to select a potential employer. On January 10, 2000, AOL announced its intention to acquire media giant Time Warner for $130 billion, creating an Internet-media powerhouse that is expected to be unrivaled for its breadth and scope in both old and new media.

Of course, stock charts do not tell an employee everything he or she needs to know about an employer. But they do provide a snapshot that shows how the company is perceived on Wall Street. It is a bottom-line-oriented snapshot that can tell a viewer whether or not the firm is enjoying financial success on its own and relative to its peers. And thanks to the Internet, the charts are immediately accessible on-line. Interested parties can access stock charts on CNBC.com. I recommend using the chart that contains the entire stock history of a company. Use the settings: standard chart, maximum time, line display, and linear setting. That will give you a clear picture of the firm's stock market history.

If available, an interested party can compare the stock chart of one company against a competing firm or against a benchmark index to gain a deeper insight into the company's standing in its industry.

I would also recommend that prospective employees review a company's financial statements to assess a company's health. Those reports are now easily accessible through the Internet. Many companies maintain updated financial information, such as quarterly and annual reports, on their own web sites.

Certainly, this exercise is no substitute for visiting a company or talking to its managers and employees to determine its suitability for you. But it is a great, quick way to see how your future employer is doing financially.

Wall Street has long known how whole industries and individual companies would fare, well before their employees ever got wind of the company's future.

Nowhere has that been more obvious than in the field of biotechnology. Biotech firms are born in relative obscurity, the dreams of a few doctors or scientists who have, in their minds, the blueprints for some truly life-changing products or services.

In recent years, the stock market has provided the financing for many of these new technologies or processes that may, one day, dramatically extend the human life span or render harmless the myriad dread diseases that flesh is heir to.

As with the Internet, the market is telling us a lot about, not just the future of medicine, but also about how well we will live and die in the future. This is surely a message that cannot be ignored.

Biotechnomania

In late 1999, shares of a sector of the stock market began to multiply faster than the cells of a newly created life form. Biotech stocks, particularly those associated with a brand new branch of medicine, genomics, proliferated on Wall Street. Their rapid growth, and even more dramatic increases, opened investors' eyes to the possibility that the world may be on the verge of some important breakthroughs in the treatment and, possibly, cure of some of the planet's most dreaded diseases.

The stellar performance of biotech stocks is testimony to the market's ability to ferret out new investment opportunities in promising fields of endeavor. In that regard, genomics represented one of the hottest new enterprises at the start of the twenty-first century.

Genomics is a branch of medical science that is dedicated to the mapping of the entire human genome in an effort to identify all the genes that make up human life and to accurately assess all their functions. The Human Genome Project, a government-funded organization charged with completing the gene map, has been hard at work for a number of years. Private enterprises, many of which are now publicly traded companies, are working even more feverishly in an effort to map the human genome and launch successful businesses that will create new drugs to prevent, treat, or cure diseases like cancer, diabetes, or other debilitating conditions before they become life threatening. One such firm, Celera, says it will finish mapping the human genome well before the Human Genome Project. It is by gaining a complete understanding of humankind's genetic makeup that all of these companies hope to achieve their lofty and profitable goals.

The more accurate and complete the mapping process, the more likely, then, that medical science can identify the potential for an individual to contract a particular illness in his or her future. The process also, theoretically, makes it easier for drug companies to better design drugs to treat specific diseases by preempting the illnesses that once caused great suffering and death.

It is easy to understand why both medical science and commercial enterprises, like big pharmaceutical companies, are so terribly excited about the field of genomics.

At the dawn of the new millenium, investors were equally enthusiastic about the prospects for revolutionary developments in this embryonic industry. And the stock prices reflected both hope and hype very early in the year.

By the end of February, the biotech index, comprised of both established biotechnology companies and some emerging firms as well, sprang to life. The index gained 100 percent in the first two months of the year. That is a bigger gain than the high flying NASDAQ Composite enjoyed in all of 1999. (As you'll recall, the tech-laden NASDAQ jumped 85 percent in 1999, the largest gain for a U.S. stock market index since early in the twentieth century.)

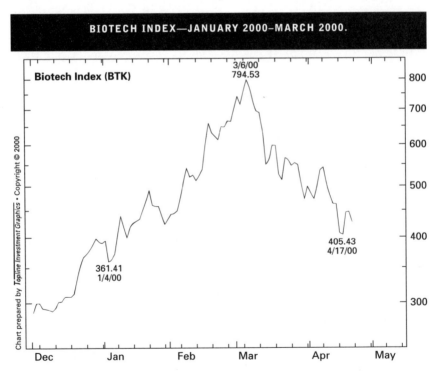

BIOTECH INDEX—JANUARY 2000–MARCH 2000.

The gains in individual biotech and genomics shares were even more astounding. Firms like Human Genome Sciences, Celera, Incyte Pharmaceuticals doubled, tripled, or quadrupled in a very short period of time, as investors bet that these firms would reap substantial rewards from their pioneering work in the field. Some companies planned to license their gene maps to larger pharmaceutical firms as the drug companies developed new products based on genomic breakthroughs. Other companies worked to patent actual genes and then profit from their "ownership" of as many genes as possible. (The patenting of genes is a business effort not fully tested. Many observers expect that there will be legal challenges to the concept of individual companies owning patents on genes, a trick that would make even Levi Strauss envious!)

But clearly, the stock market was sending a message, as it did with original biotech stocks in the early 1990s, that something very new and very important was happening in medicine as the century unfolded.

Interestingly, as investors poured more and more money into the maturing field of biotechnology and the emerging field of genomics, investment dollars were siphoned out of old-line pharmaceutical firms.

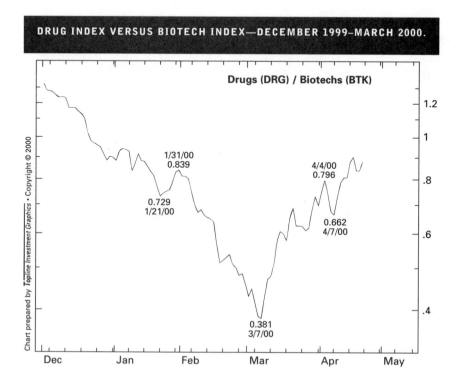

DRUG INDEX VERSUS BIOTECH INDEX—DECEMBER 1999–MARCH 2000.

Drugs (DRG) / Biotechs (BTK)

Chart prepared by *Topline Investment Graphics* • Copyright © 2000

Investors appeared to be betting that the new companies held greater promise for more rapid growth than the old drug companies, even among those with recognizable brand names like Johnson & Johnson, Merck, Pfizer (remember Viagra?), and Warner-Lambert. Indeed, the promise of growth, unverified by actual products, sales and profits, was tantalizingly large in the upstart companies. The idea of curing the most deadly diseases was as attractive as the concept of a perpetual motion machine was hundreds of years ago. Its promise was alluring until it was proved it couldn't be done. But, oftentimes, investors will pay up for the promise in the fervent hope that the rewards far outweigh the risks.

Still, the stock market was sending a signal in early 2000 that it was possible, not probable, but possible that an entirely new industry was being born. And unlike any emerging field that came before, even the Internet, this business had the potential to do what no industry has ever done before—substantially lengthen human life spans and maybe even pose a grave challenge to the notions of death and dying.

On Tuesday March 14, 2000, U.S. President Bill Clinton and his British counterpart, Tony Blair, issued a joint declaration, calling for all of the scientific data on the human genome to be made freely available to scientists all over the world.

Biotechnology stocks plunged 13 percent as a group, in many cases by far greater percentages for specific securities, amid fears that the declaration would limit the commercial viability of the 20 publicly traded genomics companies. Their future depended on their ability to either patent genes or sell their proprietary gene maps to interested parties for a substantial profit. If all genomics data were to be made freely available, then for-profit companies may not survive in such an egalitarian environment.

At the time of this book's publication, it was not known whether the industry can ever live up to its promise. It could be seriously hampered not just by the legal challenges facing companies who want to own the human genome but also by the degree of difficulty involved in creating disease-curing drugs from genetic information.

After the Terrible Tuesday in March 2000, biotech stocks were down substantially from their highs achieved earlier in the year. But they were still up 70 percent year-to-date. However, by early summer biotechnology shares had plunged further, in some cases falling as much as 75 percent. Biotech shares had suffered similar explosive rallies and subsequent declines in the early 1990s. And while investors suffered as a consequence, the field of biotechnology continued to expand and make significant contributions to modern medicine.

The market still appeared to be saying that despite some short-term volatility it's altogether possible that some day only one thing in life, rather than two, may be certain, and it won't be death—just taxes!

Only time will tell.

3

All the World's a Sage

It's not just here at home that markets send messages. Financial markets all around the world send similar signals. From Holland's buoyant tulip markets in the early 1600s to South Korea's astonishing stock market of the 1990s, markets have sent important messages throughout history, regardless of time or geography. Sometimes those messages are important only to the locals, while at other times, overseas markets send signals to be heard around the world.

Free trade and globalization have increasingly intertwined the economies and markets across the planet. Technological innovation, the invention of the computer, the advent of the Internet, and the introduction of portable wireless communication of all kinds mean that investment capital knows no boundaries. Professional and individual investors can rapidly move their money from one hot spot to another in the information age in the blink of an eye, making geography irrelevant and borders increasingly porous.

Pulitzer Prize-winning columnist Thomas L. Friedman of the *New York Times* describes that new world order in his very fine book, *The Lexus and the Olive Tree*. Friedman chronicles the rapid and seismic shift from the old world order to the new, illustrating quite clearly how the modern economy is changing the world in ways never thought possible before.

As a consequence, it is incumbent upon all of us to heed not just the message of our own markets, but of all markets. Recent economic history provides numerous object lessons in why that is true.

The collapse of Japan's stock market in 1989 heralded the end of "Japan Inc.," and set the stage for America's corporate and economic renaissance in the 1990s. The Asian currency crisis in 1997, the Russian ruble crisis, and the collapse of the Long-Term Capital hedge fund sent shock waves through all world markets, sending a message to investors and policymakers alike that unstable economic systems or market structures could threaten the entire global economy. Fortunately for all of us, policymakers acted expeditiously in the latter two cases and prevented back-to-back market meltdowns from becoming full-blown economic catastrophes.

I have discussed the market crises of 1997 and 1998 with countless experts and high-ranking policymakers. All agree that were it not for the prompt actions that were taken to ameliorate the effects of the meltdowns, the economic landscape would look wildly different in the early part of the twenty-first century than it does today.

After the Russian ruble crisis and Long-Term Capital's trillion-dollar implosion, central banks all over the world cut interest rates rapidly while countries and firms rescued troubled institutions. The rapid response saved the day.

What is most interesting, however, about the crisis of the late 1990s, is that investors should have seen them coming. The crash of Japan's stock market in 1990 sent a vivid signal to investors and local policymakers that the good times were coming to an end. Japanese officials played Nero for nearly a decade, ignoring the implications of a stock market plunge—their economy suffered for 10 years as a result.

Later in the decade, the collapse of Thailand's currency, known as the *baht,* sent a message that Asian markets and economies were at risk of a debilitating round of currency crashes. Although they ignored the message initially, investors, central bankers, and finance ministers ultimately took notice and reacted appropriately, just as they would a scant year later, when Russia's troubles threatened to destabilize the world all over again.

That the markets and economies of the world are increasingly interdependent, there is no doubt. Investors and economists, however, still sometimes doubt the validity of important messages being sent from distant lands. The lessons of the 1990s prove that no one can afford to be parochial anymore. If one is going to heed the message of the markets, one must heed the messages of all markets.

Setting Sun

There may have been no more potent message ever sent by a market than the message sent by Japan's Nikkei stock average on the final day of 1989. On that day, the Nikkei-225, Japan's version of the Dow Jones Industrial Average, hit an all-time high of 39,900. In the decade since, it has never come close to revisiting such lofty heights. In a space of a few short years, the Nikkei collapsed by 60 percent, one of the worst declines ever in Japan. Ten years later, it hadn't even climbed back to 20,000.

Its multiyear decline, the crushing bear market in stocks that lasted for the entire decade of the 1990s, told everyone from Tokyo to Tallahassee that Japan's economy was in serious trouble. But in the days when Japan Inc. reigned supreme, no one was willing to listen to the message of the Nikkei.

The crash of Japan's stock market is a stunning reminder that markets do rise and fall to extremes. It is also a reminder that extreme moves in markets contain potent information about the future and simply cannot be ignored. Such was the case in the Japan of the 1970s and 1980s.

Very few people recall where the Dow and the Nikkei were trading in the early 1970s. Both averages struggled to hold onto their first millennial mark. The Dow and the Nikkei both approached 1000 at about the same time. Both struggled to penetrate that level in a meaningful way for many years. Throughout the 1970s, both countries' economies were being ravaged by inflation and rising oil prices. Both countries were trying desperately to adapt to the puzzling and challenging economic environment of the time.

For years, those two bellwether averages accomplished precious little, just as the economies of both countries foundered. But something curious happened along the way. Even as the United States began to regain past glories with the election of Ronald Reagan in 1980 and the start of a new bull market in 1982, Japan Inc. went on a tear.

As the world economy began to recover in the early 1980s, Japan became the dominant player on the world stage. To be sure, America was enjoying her own renaissance or rebirth, but Japan was coming of age. While America *reinvented* its swashbuckling brand of capitalism, Japan *invented* capitalism anew, merging centuries old mercantilism with Asian socialism, creating a new system the West had not anticipated or ever seen.

Indeed, Japan's elder bureaucrats had put to paper a plan for world economic domination in the 1970s that mirrored its military plans composed at the start of the last century. Japan replaced its samurai warrior with a samurai CEO, using a military battle plan to engage in economic warfare.

There was a certain imperial majesty to Japan's economic power. It was bold, assertive, and combative. From its massive export platforms, Japan began to launch blistering attacks on weaker business rivals. Through its Byzantine collection of rules and regulations, it could stifle competition in its own market, giving favor to local enterprise while locking out barbarian invaders at the border. In short, in the space of less than two decades, Japan had done what it had always done best, imported capitalism from the West, adopted it, and then perfected it by bending it to its own cultural paradigms.

In the early 1980s, the world began to notice the changes taking place on the economic scene. America was indeed rising again. But in the Land of the Rising Sun, ascendancy was the watchword of the day. Informed observers of the global economy issued warning after warning about Japan Inc. Many pointed out that Tokyo's economic system was unfairly constructed to give Japan a serious competitive advantage over its larger, Western rivals.

Indeed, in addition to manufacturing vastly superior consumer products, Japan manufactured a form of financial capitalism that was, or so it seemed, vastly superior to previous models. Japan's biggest banks and manufacturing and service companies invested in one another. Banks like Mitsubishi Trust owned a chunk of Mitsubishi Industries and Mitsubishi Motors, who, in turn, owned stakes in the parent bank. These interlocking directorates, or *keiretsu,* created vast efficiencies. The bank offered discount financing to members of the Mitsubishi family. Since each family member owned a stake in the other, each benefited from the success of its corporate siblings. As the stocks of each company rose, shares of the other member companies rose in tandem, creating a daisy chain of prosperity that promised to go on forever.

This massive entanglement of good fortune blossomed throughout the country as the keiretsu benefited handsomely from renewed prosperity around the globe. Japan's big businesses exported their fine products around the world, financed inexpensively by doting parent companies. They often sold their wares at below market prices, driving out competition and grabbing market share in faraway places. The whole process was supported by an extensive network of lobbyists, propagandists, and hired guns who sold the world on Japan Inc.

So as Japan grew and prospered, so did its stock market. The Nikkei, once sitting uncomfortably at the same level as the Dow, took off with the American stock market and economy, on whose fortunes Japan's stock market and economy rested. But it didn't stop there. After pausing, in fact, plummeting with the U.S. market in 1987, the Nikkei began a period of stunning outperformance that would lead many to believe that the sun was setting on the West and rising, forever, in the East.

In the last three years of the 1980s, Japan would embark on an economic juggernaut that would make it the envy of the world. The Nikkei rebounded almost immediately after it crashed in October

1987. It would travel from a low of about 9000 that autumn to nearly 40,000 in December 1989. The Dow would recover, but not nearly as dramatically. By the time the Nikkei touched 40,000, the Dow had barely exceeded its precrash high of 2700.

Property prices in Japan surged in the final few years of the decade, reflecting the resiliency of Japan's market and economy. Office space in Tokyo was at a premium. Young Japanese men, frantic to acquire living space in Japan's business district, the Ginza, rented the equivalent of storage spaces in which to live, for thousands of dollars a month. By 1989, the sum value of real estate in Tokyo was worth more than all of the real estate in the United States! Such was the mania in Japan for stocks and property.

Morgan Stanley's chief global strategist, Barton Biggs, observed, quite presciently at the time, that no other speculative bubble in history compared to the excesses that took place in Japan in the last year of the 1980s.

Biggs's study compared Japan's bubble economy of the 1980s to previous speculative episodes in economic history and produced some staggering results.

He wrote that those episodes, like the one in Japan, often met a violent death, with asset values declining by between 50 and 90 percent. His call was right on target. From its 1989 peak of nearly 40,000, the Nikkei plunged 60 percent in a few short years, ushering in the worst recession in Japan's postwar history.

But before that debacle took place, Japan's economic star continued to rise. Japan's biggest and most successful companies roamed the planet, gobbling up real estate and other foreign firms, while opening up their own manufacturing facilities in far-off lands.

In the United States, American business leaders scrambled to curry favor with the new samurai in pin-striped suits. Trade experts railed about Japan's rapacious appetite for acquisitions. Members of Congress howled about Tokyo's unfair trade practices. Journalists and novelists bashed Japan for its perceived arrogance and ambitions to rule the economic world.

In the autumn of 1990, best-selling author and moviemaker

Michael Crichton published *Rising Sun*. Using a murder mystery as a backdrop, Crichton raised serious questions about an America whose fortunes had suddenly sagged under the weight of Japanese competition. The novel exposed American economic weaknesses, examined Japan's newfound supremacy, and exposed the unfair advantage Japan Inc. had acquired through the magic of financial engineering. His stinging criticisms of the United States for its laziness and Japan for its hubris would hit the shelves just as Japan's stock market hit its peak. The novel served not only as a wake-up call for the West but also as a death knell for the East.

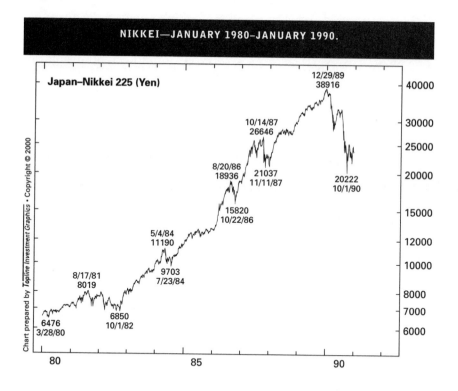

Japan's orgy of speculation in stocks, bonds, real estate, and luxury goods hit its terminal point on December 31, 1989. The Nikkei nicked 40,000 as Tokyo's bulls forecast a never ending run that would drive the Nikkei to 100,000, if not higher. But that was not to be.

Amid sharp criticism from its major trading partners, like the United States, the United Kingdom, and Germany, the Bank of Japan took steps to prick the bubble in Japan in an effort to deflate the markets without destroying the economy. Many economists around the world argued that the unending rise in stock and property prices in Japan left its economy vulnerable to a market crash, a crash that would destabilize Japan's economy and drag the rest of the world into a recession or worse.

They were partly right. As the Bank of Japan raised interest rates to stop the rampant inflation in asset prices, the Nikkei stopped going up. Real estate values peaked and then began to slide. As Japan's central banks tightened monetary policy, Japan's financial markets showed just how vulnerable they were to a deep downturn. The Nikkei, in the space of a few short years, plunged 60 percent in value.

The crash of Japan's stock market revealed the serious flaws in

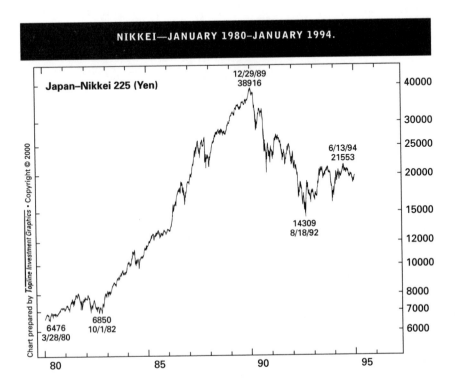

NIKKEI—JANUARY 1980–JANUARY 1994.

Tokyo's master economic plan. As both stock and property prices plunged, banks were suddenly buried under a mountain of bad debts. Since banks owned stock in their subsidiary companies, and counted their stockholdings as capital, they found themselves suddenly and shockingly undercapitalized. Japan's big and small banks had also aggressively financed the real estate boom of the 1980s. The subsequent crash left them holding either valueless mortgages or pieces of property that were persistently plunging in value.

The daisy chain of cross-holdings that had supported stock prices when times were good turned into a death spiral for many Japanese corporations. As their investments in affiliated companies sank, so did the value of their own stock. International Strategy & Investment's Jason Trennert notes that despite their vaunted efficiencies and world class production methods, Japanese corporations did not produce high rates of return on their equity. Return on equity was only 5 percent. The divergence between rates of return and the performance of Japanese equities was a key sign of an unstable system. It was a nightmare scenario that resembled the nightmare the United States endured in the late 1920s and early 1930s.

The crash of the Nikkei sent a message to Japan that the party was indeed over. Just as the flappers of the Jazz Age could no longer sip champagne from their shoes, the samurai CEOs of the Japan Age could no longer pay $20 for an American apple or $100 for a piece of aged American beef.

And just as America received an alarming message from Wall Street in 1929, Japan received a stern warning from its stock market some 60 years later.

The bursting of Japan's stock market bubble sent the Japanese economy into a tailspin. Almost immediately after stock prices began their 10-year descent, real estate prices began to collapse. Over the next several years, Tokyo property prices plunged. Office space, which once sold at a premium, would eventually decline in value by about 60 to 70 percent. Very few Japanese companies recognized the price declines on their books, which had the unwanted effect of extending the bad times. (As U.S. real estate investors found out in the 1980s, the more quickly one recognizes a loss and writes it off, the more quickly the bear market in property comes to an end.)

The plunge in real estate values pressured Japan's banks, big and small. The once mighty lenders were all too happy to finance real estate speculation in Japan, and like their American counterparts from the 1980s, many of Japan's banks would go bust in the 1990s.

Almost as suddenly as the market dropped, Japan Inc. began to go bankrupt. The bankruptcy of Japan's economy would take years to unfold, a decade to be exact, but it was presaged by that 60 percent tumble in the value of the Nikkei-225.

Japan was however, in many ways, quite different than the United States in the 1930s. Japan's corporations promised lifetime employment while the government offered generous social safety nets to those in need. So while Japan's population never suffered the misery of their American predecessors, Japan's economic machine certainly did.

Faced with massive capital losses in the stock market, a slowdown in consumer spending, heavy debt burdens, and rising costs, Japan's biggest corporations and banks plunged deeply into the red. By the mid-1990s, the once proud keiretsu companies were reporting staggering losses in the billions of dollars. Names like Mitsubishi, NEC, Sony, and Matsushita suffered a humbling loss of face. The banks also were shamed. It was not uncommon for humiliated bankers and corporate executives to take their own lives as things went from bad to worse. By 1997, it was reported that the suicide rate among Japanese executives had climbed to one a day.

Japan's ability to finance its own economic recovery ground to a halt. The nation's big banks reeled under mountains of bad debt, while falling stock prices eroded their capital sharply. In the biggest bank merger in the history of the world, the Bank of Tokyo was forced to merge with Mitsubishi Bank. The Tokyo government simply arranged the marriage of two struggling banks in hopes of creating one strong one. Other such "shotgun" mergers became commonplace.

As the markets and economy continued their seemingly endless death spiral, Japan's top policymakers made matters worse by choosing the wrong policy prescriptions every step of the way.

The Bank of Japan, long after it was necessary to do so, kept interest rates far too high. It popped the speculative bubble in the stock and real estate markets, but its restrictive policies remained in place until the real economy suffered, as well. Japan's chief central banker failed to learn the lessons the Americans suffered through in the late 1920s and early 1930s.

Additionally, Japan's ruling Liberal Democratic Party stumbled through a series of scandals, beginning in the early 1990s, scandals that exposed just how corrupt the country's government truly was. Bribery scandals and stock scams were uncovered. Many politicians were linked to crooked businessmen. Many politicians unfairly profited from inside stock deals that were common in the great bull market of the 1980s. As a consequence, Japan started going through governments faster than many small Latin American nations. The uncertainty engendered by the constant state of political flux prevented the government from passing any stimulative programs that could have lessened the ravages of recession or shortened its duration.

In early 1999, Japan's economy was still in recession. Corporations there suffered the ill effects of falling prices for their goods and services, a pernicious condition known as deflation. In Japan, deflation was renamed *price destruction.* In many ways that moniker describes far more accurately the condition we call *deflation.*

Despite some halfhearted measures to stimulate the economy and a delayed response to lower interest rates by the Bank of Japan, price destruction continued for over a decade in Tokyo, just as it had in the United States some 60 years earlier.

It was only in mid-1999 that Japanese policymakers began to make a serious effort to redress the situation. Bad banks were closed or merged aggressively. Corporations wrote off bad debts, laid off workers, and restructured their organizations. Japan's hobbled government finally passed a massive stimulus program while the Bank of Japan flooded the economy with money.

As the millennium drew to a close, Japan's economy began to grow again.

Had Japan's leaders and stodgy bureaucrats heeded the message of their own market, the sun may have never set on the land of the rising sun. Indeed, Japan's ascendancy to the top spot in the world economy may have ushered in the Asian Century a decade before it was supposed to begin.

Those devastating troubles that began for Japan at the start of the 1990s sowed the seeds of destruction for all of Asia about seven years later.

As Japan's economy deflated throughout the early 1990s, Japanese investors started pulling in their reins. They brought as much money home as they could, selling off their profitable overseas investments to cover losses at home. That tidal flow of funds back to Tokyo, a tsunami if you will, put great upward pressure on the Japanese yen, and greatly weakened the U.S. dollar.

By April 1995, the dollar was collapsing against the yen. So great was the distress that policymakers from the United States and Japan, led by Treasury Secretary Robert Rubin, intervened to support the dollar. The intervention was quite successful and in the space of two years, the dollar appreciated rapidly against the yen. Or to put it another way, the yen was devalued against the dollar.

The devaluation of the yen was an important economic event that led to still greater troubles in the region. True, a strong yen created problems of its own. The rapid appreciation of the yen had previously put immense pressure on Japan's rapidly deflating economy. (A stronger yen just increased the deflationary pressures.) But the decline of the yen caused wider troubles still.

Since most of Asia's other currencies were pegged to the U.S. dollar, as the dollar rose against the yen, it also rose against all the currencies of the Pacific Rim. The problem was not that the dollar was rising but that the exchange rate systems of Thailand, Indonesia, Malaysia, Singapore, and elsewhere were rigid and inflexible. As the dollar rose, something had to give. Either the governments of the Asian nations had to raise interest rates to stabilize the falling values of their currencies or they had to cut their currencies loose from their ties to the dollar. Heady stuff to be sure. But it was amid this tension that the Asian currency crisis of 1997 exploded into a full-blown global affair.

This worldwide panic should not have been a surprise. A clear warning was given before the crisis spun out of control.

The Baht Heard 'Round the World

By late 1997, nearly all of Asia was in recession, and by early 1998, was in depression, the most severe economic contraction of the post–World War II era. Few, if any, average Asians ever saw this catastrophe coming. Even fewer Americans, a parochial lot at best, even knew where some of the affected countries could be found on a map. And yet, this massive economic event meant almost as much to the average American as it did to the average Asian.

While the Asians suffered greatly because of this calamity, Americans, by and large, prospered. It is safe to say, however, that neither the average Asian nor the average American was prescient enough to recognize the signs of impending disaster that would strike the world's financial markets like a bolt from the blue. But as always, there were warning signs. And as always, very few people paid attention to the yellow lights flashing from Manhattan to Malaysia.

Simply put, the collapse of a little currency known as the Thai baht would signal the onset of a two-year recession in Asia. The signal was sent loudly and clearly, but only a few smart investors and a few smart locals ever received the message.

The story of Asia in the 1980s and early 1990s was nothing short of remarkable. The newly industrialized countries of the Pacific Rim, or NICS as they were known, were the pride of the region. So fast was their growth, so magnificent were the accomplishments, that they were nicknamed the *Asian tigers,* a group that included Thailand, Malaysia, Indonesia, Singapore, and South Korea. The Philippines also enjoyed similar status, though to a lesser extent, owing to the persistent political chaos in the post-Marcos years.

Hong Kong was also a member of the group, and in fact, one of the most dynamic economies among them, despite its small size. According to the International Monetary Fund (IMF), growth in the five main "tiger" countries averaged 8 percent per year until the crisis hit. In the previous 30 years, per capita income levels rose tenfold in Korea, fivefold in Thailand, and fourfold in Malaysia. Hong Kong and Singapore boasted income levels higher than in some fully developed nations of the West. The region, because of its phenomenal growth, attracted Western investors in droves. In 1996, they poured $100 billion into non-Japan Asia (13).

Indeed, the IMF's managing director, Stanley Fischer, addressing a group of bankers in January of 1998, called Asia's growth record prior to the crisis "unprecedented, a remarkable historic achievement" (14).

So why was it that most investors, all the world's politicians, and nearly an entire region's population failed to notice trouble signs on the horizon? It certainly wasn't that those yellow warning lights weren't flashing. Once again, it was the failure of many observers to pay attention to the market's ominous message.

In July 1997, that message emanated from a most unlikely place, the exotic capital city of Thailand—Bangkok.

The devaluation of an obscure currency known as the Thai baht that month was a nonevent outside the currency trading rooms of the world's great financial centers. In the $1 trillion worth of currency transactions handled daily, the volume of trading in the Thai baht was relatively insignificant. On most days, traders talked more about the value of the U.S. dollar, British pound, Japanese yen, or German mark than they did about the small currencies of South and East Asia. Outside those trading rooms, the rest of the world didn't discuss currency exchange rates at all.

Indeed, as I was told by the producer of a popular morning television program who had asked me to keep simple my explanation of the deepening Asian currency crisis later that year, "Remember, most of my viewers don't even know Thailand *has* a currency."

Even some editors at respectable business news organizations failed to grasp the significance of the crisis and were heard to mutter to a plaintive reporter pitching a currency crisis story:

"Why do I care?"

In a matter of months, the answer to that intellectually lazy question would be answered with a vengeance.

But it was against that backdrop that the world's currency markets were sending a message to Asia and to the entire world to prepare for a significant economic event.

On July 2, 1997, the Thai government devalued its currency, the baht. In the financial markets, this truly was the baht heard 'round the world, though its reverberations on the main streets of the world would be heard only many months later. But the baht's plunge in value was indeed a significant event. The precipitous nature of its decline was striking in both speed and scope, as the chart clearly illustrates.

Some market participants understood clearly the meaning of

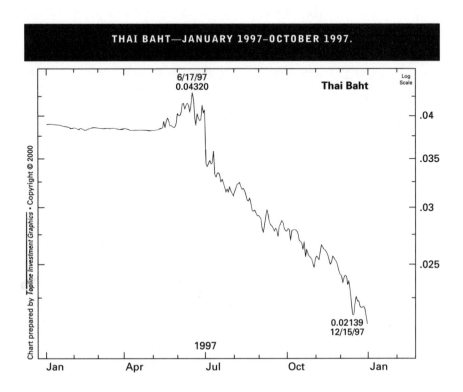

THAI BAHT—JANUARY 1997–OCTOBER 1997.

the message. Billionaire money manager George Soros not only understood the significance of the baht's devaluation, he participated in it, profiting handsomely from the currency's crash against the dollar. Soros saw, with foresight, what many economists and lesser market players saw only with hindsight—that the rapid pace of growth in that country, in that region, was unsustainable. And that the instability, caused by rapid growth, would have a significant impact on the value of the currencies in question.

To understand why that is true, an explanation of the region's foreign exchange system is required. Many countries of the developing world tie the values of their currencies to that of the U.S. dollar. By "fixing" foreign exchange rates and eliminating fluctuations in the value of their currencies, developing countries can maintain smooth trade flows with big countries like the United States. Instead of suffering wild swings in the value of exported goods, smaller countries with pegged exchange rates can even out the income they receive from exporting goods and maintain a more healthy economy. That assumes, of course, that all other economic developments are favorable or, at least, stable.

But those very unstable elements were, for a time, the driving forces behind the rapid pace of economic growth. As the region prospered and grew quickly through mammoth exports of cheap consumer goods to the region, Western investors poured hundreds of billions of dollars into Asia's fast-rising markets. The more money Asia attracted, the higher the markets went. The higher their stock markets went, the more wealth was created inside each of these newly industrialized countries. The greater the wealth, the more careless domestic investors and big financial institutions became.

In Indonesia and Malaysia the race was on to build the world's tallest and longest buildings. The "hot money" of the West helped to finance these speculative real estate ventures. Indonesian and Malaysian banks, flush with cash, financed all manner of wild projects, from real estate ventures to businesses run by friends and family of the two nations' ruling families. In Korea, huge conglomerates known as *chaebols* were engaging in similarly incestuous practices, rapidly expanding their spheres of influence as they grew into unwieldy, inefficient enterprises. In the wake of Asia's collapse, this brand of economic activity would be branded *crony capitalism,* and would mar the respectability of Asia's economic boom, so lauded by Western investors for many years.

The excesses engendered by crony capitalism would create stresses in the financial systems throughout the Pacific Rim. As economic growth inevitably slowed, the returns on uneconomic investments began to shrink. Asia's export machine slowed down in early 1997, creating dangerously large trade deficits for nearly every country in the group.

Suddenly, Asia's tiger economies looked more like domesticated cats, smaller, less aggressive, and far more tame. This quick shift in the relative performance of Asian economies led to a reassessment on the part of Western investors who began to pull their money out of the region, selling their Asian investments and converting them back into dollars, deutsche marks, or pounds. Asian investors, sensing that the jig was up, began moving their own money offshore to safer places like Switzerland.

Even members of the ruling Suharto family in Indonesia were rumored to have been funneling money out of their country as it became increasingly apparent that an economic crisis was simmering.

Just as a massive inflow of capital had boosted the region's economies in years past, a rapid flight of capital from Asia put a major strain on the economies of the Pac Rim.

Something had to give. And that something was the value of the currency.

So, after defending the value of the Thai baht in the early summer of 1997 by raising interest rates to attract foreign investment, the government of Thailand abandoned its efforts to fix the value of the baht.

On July 2, the Thai government let the currency trade freely against the U.S. dollar. The baht promptly plunged in value by 20 percent in a single day. It would fall far further before the Asian currency crisis would run its course.

George Soros, who quietly assessed the troubles of Thailand, would make nearly $1 billion betting that the Thai baht would be devalued. (Soros earned his legendary reputation as a world-class financier only a few years earlier. In 1992, he correctly bet that the British government would devalue the British pound despite the Bank of England's solid promise to defend the value of the pound sterling. Soros, in his speculative endeavors, "broke the bank," earning a cool billion in the process.)

Other investors failed to heed the message that Soros and the baht were sending. Since many of Asia's tiger economies had weaknesses similar to those of Thailand—slowing growth, yawning trade deficits, speculative booms in both stock and real estate markets—it meant that their economies and their currencies were vulnerable to similar calamities.

Speculators launched raids against the fixed currencies of Indonesia, Malaysia, Singapore, South Korea, and the Philippines. The currency pegs, after brief attempts by those nations' central banks to defend them, snapped like little twigs. The currencies of every Asian tiger plummeted in value.

The Indonesian rupiah, the Malaysian ringgit, the Philippine peso, the Singapore dollar, and the Korean won collapsed.

Interest rates across Asia soared. Economic activity in the world's fastest-growing countries shut down instantly. Stock markets crashed from Singapore to Seoul. Leading financial officials of the United States told some reporters privately that the destruction of wealth in emerging Asia was without precedent in modern economic history. The speed with which markets collapsed surpassed that of the 1929 crash. It was a crushing blow to the people of Asia, who until only weeks before, were enjoying an unprecedented wave of prosperity. The Asian Contagion, as it was quickly dubbed in the financial press, spread like wildfire, laying waste the Pacific Rim's stock and bond markets and ravaging every economy outside of China and Japan.

The tsunami in the Far Eastern markets had a measurable ripple effect on markets in the Western world. On October 27, 1997, the

Dow Jones Industrial Average plunged a record 554 points, the largest single-day point decline in Wall Street's history. (While the Dow's drop was a record point loss, it paled in comparison to the record 22.7 percent collapse 10 years earlier on Black Monday, 1987.)

Veteran hedge fund speculator Victor Neiderhoffer, a well-respected money manager and world-class squash champion, was wiped out that very day. Even George Soros, who had profited so handsomely from the crash of the Thai baht, took a bath on Wall Street that Monday afternoon, losing $1 billion in a single session.

Investors in the United States braced for the worst, expecting that Asia's coming depression would quickly spread to the Western world. At its low point, the Dow declined nearly 20 percent from its most recent all-time high. Technology stocks, many of which exported large quantities of goods to Asia, slumped in value. Many semiconductor manufacturers, whose business was largely dependent on a strong Pacific Rim, suffered declines that lasted two years. Those recessions only recently had run their course. Mutual funds that invested in Asian nations were badly beaten down and stayed down for years afterward.

In Asia, aid was desperately needed and the West rallied to help. The International Monetary Fund, financed principally by the United States and other big, industrial powers, lent countless billions of dollars to the struggling region. Thailand, the trigger point for the currency crisis, was granted $17.2 billion in emergency loans. Indonesia and Malaysia received nearly $60 billion between them. South Korea also was rescued. All of the money came in exchange for promises of structural economic reforms in the countries that practiced crony capitalism.

Despite the rescue, and the attempts at reform, the collapse took a serious human toll on citizens throughout the Far East. Plunging currencies caused inflation to skyrocket, driving up the price of the most important commodity—food. In Indonesia, the largest country among the defanged tigers, citizens could not afford rice or even cooking oil. Press reports at the time estimated that by

December 1997, almost half of the nation's 200 million people were going hungry on a regular basis. Riots broke out across the country. Hundreds, even thousands, died in clashes with police. A state of emergency was declared, martial law imposed, and curfews were brutally enforced. The 30-year-old government of President Suharto fell, as did governments in Thailand and South Korea. Even Japan was not spared. The world's second largest economy, still reeling from its own economic crisis, suffered further as the depression abroad exacerbated its recession at home. Japan's prime minister, Ryutaro Hashimoto, was unceremoniously booted from office.

In the West, the tsunami never hit the mainland directly. Instead, Asia's bust, surprisingly, turned into America's boom. The collapse in Asian currencies, markets, and economies flattened the demand for important commodities like crude oil, computer products, grains, and lumber. As a consequence, the cost of gasoline in the United States fell to its lowest price ever, in inflation-adjusted terms. Recall that prices for gas dropped to less than $1 per gallon in some parts of the country as the crisis played itself out for over a year.

Inflation fell to its lowest level in 30 years for American consumers. Interest rates dropped accordingly, touching off a rapid acceleration in home purchases, mortgage refinancings, and other interest rate–sensitive activity. The U.S. economy boomed even as other economies suffered their worst performances of the postwar period.

Federal Reserve Chairman Alan Greenspan was among the first to recognize that Asia's loss would be America's gain. In congressional testimony in the winter of 1997, the sage central banker noted that the startling events of the previous few months would likely have a "salutary" effect on the U.S. economy. He was right. America's gross domestic product expanded by more than 4 percent in 1997, while inflation fell to nearly negligible levels. The stock market rebounded smartly and went on to new highs by mid-1998.

The crisis, while a lingering and large concern for economic policymakers, faded from the nation's consciousness in a relatively

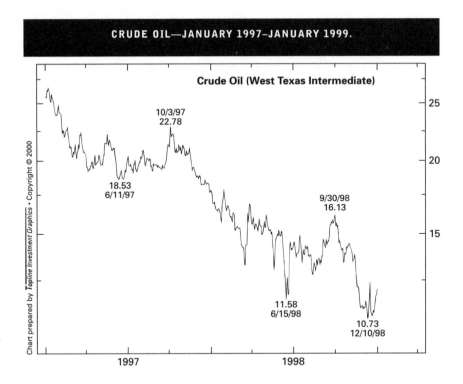

CRUDE OIL—JANUARY 1997–JANUARY 1999.

Crude Oil (West Texas Intermediate)

10/3/97
22.78

18.53
6/11/97

9/30/98
16.13

11.58
6/15/98

10.73
12/10/98

25

20

15

1997   1998

Chart prepared by *Topline Investment Graphics* • Copyright © 2000

short period of time. It would rear its ugly head again in a matter of months, as the next dominoes would begin to fall in the summer of 1998.

World financial markets began to heal themselves in early 1998. Investors grew increasingly confident that "the committee to save the world," as *Time* magazine dubbed Alan Greenspan, Treasury Secretary Robert Rubin, and his deputy, Larry Summers, had done just that. The rapid response team, through the good offices of the IMF and the World Bank, had rescued Asia or, at the very least, had turned the tide of the biggest tsunami ever to threaten Asia's shores (15).

The battered currencies of Thailand, Indonesia, Malaysia, and South Korea had stopped falling. Financial markets stabilized to some degree, though they were still vulnerable to tremors and after-shocks inspired by the shake-up of only a few months before.

But by January, it appeared that policymakers were gaining the upper hand. A sense of calm was returning to world markets. It was tentative at best. But at the time, a tentative calm was the best anyone could hope for. That calm would last for only a few months before the world economy would be thrown into another maelstrom, this one more threatening to the West than the one that came before. And this one would require direct intervention by the U.S. Federal Reserve, using its most potent weapon, interest rate reductions, to save the U.S. economy from certain disaster.

And this time, only obscure market indicators would warn of impending calamity. The warnings spoke quite plainly. The only problem for most investors was that they didn't even know where to look.

Ruble Roulette

About as soon as the immediate global threat from the Asian currency crisis subsided, investors returned to making risky bets in the emerging stock, bond, and currency markets of the Western world. Asia was shunned, of course, having recently handed global portfolio managers sizable losses, a sin for which there is no forgiveness in financial circles. And while investors rarely forgive, they do often forget, which they quickly did in 1998, turning their attention from the massacre in Malaysia to the money markets of Moscow.

In less than one year's time, another major economic calamity was about to unfold, this time in an area that for nearly seven decades had shunned the outside world and had rejected the Western world's view of economics. The signal for this catastrophe also was sent from the currency markets, as investors all around the world played roulette with Russia's ruble.

By 1998, Russia's capital city had become the hub of capitalism in the former Soviet Empire. Bustling with newly minted industrialists, hot shot stock traders, and eager entrepreneurs, Moscow was fast becoming the Manhattan of Eastern Europe, or so it seemed. (Others would insist it was more like the lawless Chicago of the 1930s.)

Since 1995, many American investors had taken notice of

Russia's remarkable move toward a market economy and a social democracy. They often failed to notice, however, the absence of an ironclad constitution, the rule of law, the presence of an efficient judicial system, or a body of market regulations. Nevertheless, Western investors flocked to Moscow in droves in search of tantalizing rates of return on Russian securities. Russian T-bills offered interest rates of more than 20 percent. The Russian stock market had gone up an astonishing 250 percent between 1995 and early 1998. And for foreign investors, such mouthwatering yields were too enticing to pass up. With Russia's currency, the ruble, pegged to the value of the dollar, investors needn't have feared any currency risk, either, that could have diminished those returns when they repatriated their profits.

Wall Street had no trouble selling Russia's promising story to clients who, having been burned in Asia, wanted a fresh foreign land in which to speculate. Russian mutual funds proliferated, promising lofty returns with little risk. Sophisticated hedge fund investors, like George Soros and Leon Cooperman, a Wall Street veteran known for his searing analytical abilities, poured billions of dollars into Russian investments. Soros preached publicly about the need to help Russia make the difficult leap from 70 years of stultifying communism to a more dynamic form of capitalism. Other investors followed his lead. In fact, the hedge funds with the best rates of return in the mid-1990s invested solely in Russia, leveraging their bets in the Russian bond market and delivering triple-digit gains to their partners.

Even in the summer of 1998, when Russia's economy and markets began to falter, few observers or participants in global finance ever feared that the Asian contagion would make its way overland from Mongolia to Moscow. They were wrong and, once again, failed to hear the market's message.

The most obvious sign of impending trouble came directly from the Russian stock market. The benchmark R-T-S index began to weaken in spring of 1998, months before talk of trouble began to swing the market's pendulum from greed to fear.

RUSSIAN STOCK MARKET (RTS)—JANUARY 1995–AUGUST 1998.

Moscow Times Index

Log Scale

Chart prepared by *Topline Investment Graphics* · Copyright © 2000

8/7/97
1142

3/10/98
734

2/19/97
642

546
4/7/97

540
1/29/98

7/4/96
351

7/7/95
196

118
11/3/95

104
2/10/95

173
8/28/98

1000
700
500
300
200
150
100

1995   1996   1997   1998

Western investors also failed to note that Russian oligarchs, Moscow's modern-day equivalent of robber barons, were siphoning billions of dollars offshore into Swiss bank accounts and real estate on the French Riviera. A 1998 report from the Center for Strategic and International Studies showed that Russia's big businessmen and organized crime figures took more than $300 billion out of the country in the mid-1990s, essentially raping the Russian economy, even as Western investors were pouring billions into Russian investments.

In the late summer of 1999, the U.S. Justice Department and the U.S. Congress began investigations into a Russian money laundering scheme as well, amid allegations that unsavory characters laundered tens of billions of dollars through European and American banks. Included in the investigation was one of America's oldest lending institutions, the Bank of New York. Some of the laundered money had allegedly been taken from IMF loans, granted to Russia in the wake of their financial collapse.

Despite that disturbing fact, maybe partially because of it, Russia's economy had suffered in the aftermath of Asia's deepening recession. The price of oil, Russia's most important export, had fallen precipitously in prior months, robbing Russia of much needed hard currency revenue it received from selling oil to its principal trading partners.

The loss of revenue to the state forced the Russian government to borrow more and more money to finance its existing operations. Even as Russia attempted to transform itself from a socialist state, it had long-standing financial and burdensome financial obligations from days gone by. It still paid the salaries of restive soldiers in a dispirited military and covered the pensions of Soviet-era retirees, many of whom relied solely on the government for their subsistence.

Russia's budget deficit exploded as Moscow went on a borrowing binge. Foreign investors were all too happy to finance the Russian government's debt, accepting in return higher and higher rates of interest. As rates rose, business activity in Russia slowed to a crawl.

Pressure on the economy continued to build until Russia could no longer fix the value of the ruble to the U.S. dollar. Something had to give. Only a year after Asia's currency crisis shocked the world economy, a second currency crisis was looming on the horizon.

Despite all the pressures that were building again in the financial markets, investors remained in denial. They ignored the warning signs emanating from the Russian markets themselves. The Russian government insisted that it would not devalue the ruble, even as speculators mounted attacks against the currency on the Moscow money markets. Russian President Boris Yeltsin pledged that a devaluation would and could never happen. His prime minister and his finance minister frantically "talked up" the ruble in an effort to restore calm to the financial markets.

In the West, investors ignored some obscure but important signals that Russia was going bust and that the entire Western financial system could be at risk.

Credit spreads were widening quickly in the U.S. bond market. The yield differentials between the safest investments in the world, U.S. Treasury bonds (T-bonds), and of more risky credit instruments like corporate bonds, mortgage bonds, and emerging market debt widened to levels not seen since Orange County, California, went bankrupt in late 1994. To astute observers, widening credit spreads were a sign of panic in the financial markets.

In times of impending trouble, the smart money crowd buys U.S. Treasury bonds and sells more risky securities, reducing its tolerance for risk. In short, they flee to the relative safety of dollar-denominated assets. Since U.S. bonds are guaranteed by the "full faith and credit" of Uncle Sam, the risk of loss is minimized. So, as with nearly every financial market crisis in modern times, investors embark on a "flight to quality." Such was the case in the summer of 1998.

Those flight to quality rallies have consequences, however, in the financial markets. The massive purchases of bonds drove down the yields on T-bonds and pushed up the yields on other types of bonds. (As bond prices rise, the yield, or interest rate, on the bonds falls.) And by shunning investments in riskier type bonds, like Russian government bonds, those yields spiked ever higher, widening the gulf between U.S. bonds and all other credit instruments.

These charts depict the dramatic movement in credit spreads in the summer of 1998.

Even before it became obvious that Russia was about to become the latest victim of the Asian economic crisis, credit spreads were flashing not a yellow warning, but a red stop light.

Investors around the world, particularly the smart money crowd, were becoming averse to risk, any kind of risk. It was there for all to see, but only a few savvy players bothered to accept the message the credit markets were sending.

Shortly after these spreads widened to record levels, Russia devalued its ruble and even did the unthinkable. It defaulted on its foreign debt. Western investors, clearly stung by the devaluation, had far bigger problems than a currency crisis. The Russian government admitted that it would not pay them the interest nor principal

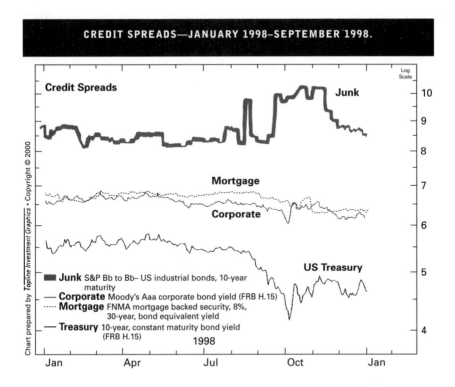

CREDIT SPREADS—JANUARY 1998–SEPTEMBER 1998.

Credit Spreads

Junk

Mortgage

Corporate

US Treasury

Junk S&P Bb to Bb– US industrial bonds, 10-year maturity
— **Corporate** Moody's Aaa corporate bond yield (FRB H.15)
····· **Mortgage** FNMA mortgage backed security, 8%, 30-year, bond equivalent yield
— **Treasury** 10-year, constant maturity bond yield (FRB H.15)

1998

Jan   Apr   Jul   Oct   Jan

Log Scale

Chart prepared by *Topline Investment Graphics* · Copyright © 2000

owed on Russian T-bills. Remember, many yield-hungry hedge funds had recently purchased Russian government bills and bonds, capturing interest rates as high as 25 percent per year!

Suddenly, not only were their investments reduced in value by the ruble's 50 percent decline, they were not going to get any money back at all. The Russian markets seized up. The Moscow Stock Exchange went into free fall. The R-T-S Index, once among the best-performing markets in the world, would decline by over 90 percent in less than one year.

Economists in the United States promised that the Russian debacle would have virtually no impact on the U.S. markets or the economy. The United States did very little trade with mother Russia. Two-way trade, in fact, was almost nonexistent. How could the United States be hurt by a country to which it had no economic ties, they asked?

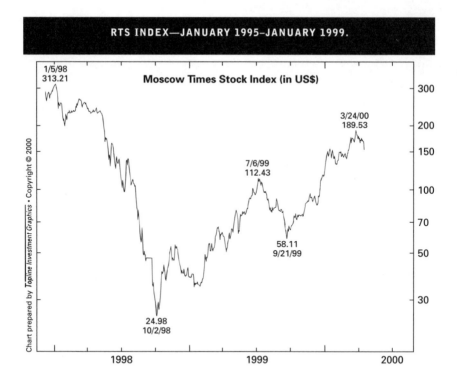

RTS INDEX—JANUARY 1995–JANUARY 1999.

Moscow Times Stock Index (in US$)

1/5/98
313.21

3/24/00
189.53

7/6/99
112.43

58.11
9/21/99

24.98
10/2/98

Chart prepared by *Topline Investment Graphics* · Copyright © 2000

1998   1999   2000

   Not only did most economists fail to listen to the message of
the market, they also failed to do their homework. Western
investors were the principal holders of worthless Russian paper.
Those high-yielding Russian T-bills were scarcely more valuable
than the czarist bonds of a century earlier. And to make matters
worse, Wall Street's financial engineers created fancy derivative
products based on Russian investments that plunged in value as the
crisis unfolded. Some market participants estimated that some
$200 billion worth of derivatives collapsed in the wake of Russia's
crisis. The financial calamity in capitalism's newest market took an
increasingly heavy toll on the West.

   One of the biggest losers in Russia's sea of red was none other
than George Soros himself. The financier and his chief lieutenant,
Stanley Druckenmiller, portfolio manager of Soros's flagship Quan-
tum Fund, had invested billions of dollars in Russia. On August 26,
Druckenmiller owned up to the losses in an interview with me on

CNBC's *Street Signs.* Druckenmiller confessed that the multi-billion-dollar fund had taken a $2 billion hit. It was an embarrassing admission from the world's savviest investor who had made billions betting against unstable countries, like Russia, in the not too distant past.

Back home, the U.S. stock market began a precipitous decline that would drive the Dow Jones Industrial Average from a summertime peak of over 10,000 to nearly 7400 by early October.

The panic, however, was not confined to the stock market. The summer of 1998 was the summer of discontent from Wall Street all the way to Washington. Imbedded in the credit market's message in mid-1998 was an event even more catastrophic than Russia's economic collapse. It was an event that would threaten the very hub of capitalism itself: the U.S. financial system.

Short Term Capital

In the wake of Russia's economic collapse, some market participants thought the U.S. markets would bounce back relatively quickly, even as some large investment funds and brokerage houses suffered sizable losses from their Russian investments. Despite that debacle, the U.S. economy was growing at a rapid pace in the summer of 1998, with few signs of inflation. While corporate profit growth began to stall, it did not force companies to slash payrolls and precipitate a recession. Instead, the lingering aftereffects of market turmoil everywhere else in the world were still keeping a lid on U.S. inflation and interest rates. Goods and services were quite affordable. Jobs were plentiful. Salaries were rising. And while stock prices were suffering, many people still had handsome paper profits on their stock market investments.

But the markets were forecasting an abrupt end to the good times here at home. Credit spreads, which had exploded with Russia's devaluation and debt default, stayed wide. It was nearly an inexplicable phenomenon. The bad news about Russia was already out. So why were the credit markets still warning of even greater trouble to come?

The answer would come from an elite conclave in Connecticut, in the small, but wealthy, hamlet known as Greenwich.

Long-Term Capital Management (LTCM) was a sophisticated investment fund for rich, well-heeled investors who were ready, willing, and able to take more risk with their investable funds. Run by a veteran Salomon Brothers bond maven, John Meriweather, a former Federal Reserve vice chair, and two Nobel laureates, LTCM raised billions of dollars to invest as it saw fit.

While its complicated strategies are difficult to explain, the principal goal of this hedge fund was to profit from small discrepancies in the prices of all manner of bonds, from U.S. Treasury bonds, to mortgage securities, to bonds of foreign governments. The hope was that the differences would eventually narrow and that LTCM's investment actions would allow it to profit as the various bonds converged in price. Long-Term Capital had made huge profits in the mid-1990s engaging in "convergence trades." That remained true until the spring and summer of 1998.

As we discussed before, the Russian debt crisis prompted investors all over the world to flock to the safety of U.S. Treasury bonds, parking money safely in a risk-free investment. As bond prices surged amid the massive inflow of funds, 30-year bond yields dropped to the lowest level in modern times.

The interest rate on the bellwether bond fell to 4.7 percent. And as rates on Treasury bonds fell precipitously, yields on other forms of bonds spiked higher, widening the spreads between both price and yield. Long-Term Capital's big bets on convergence quickly imploded in value. Rather than converge, bonds diverged and destroyed the value of LTCM's portfolio.

Now, all this would not have been so devastating had Long-Term Capital not leveraged its bond bets with billions of dollars of borrowed money. At its peak, LTCM, through the use of borrowed funds and risky derivative products, had amassed a portfolio of investments that had a face value of over $1 trillion—$1 trillion! That's roughly one-eighth the size of America's total gross domestic product.

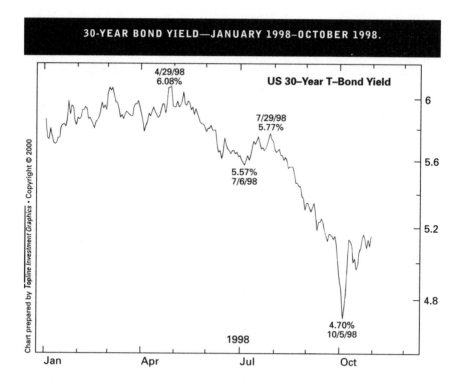

30-YEAR BOND YIELD—JANUARY 1998–OCTOBER 1998.

Chart prepared by *Topline Investment Graphics* · Copyright © 2000

US 30–Year T–Bond Yield

4/29/98
6.08%

7/29/98
5.77%

5.57%
7/6/98

4.70%
10/5/98

1998

Jan   Apr   Jul   Oct

6

5.6

5.2

4.8

Many of Wall Street's most well-respected investors and institutions, not to mention big banks, had either invested with Long-Term Capital Management or had lent the fund money to help it leverage its bets. In an instant, the U.S. financial system was exposed to the massive liabilities incurred by a single investment fund, whose trillion-dollar investment portfolio was plunging uncontrollably in value.

The U.S. stock market swooned further. The credit markets seized up. Investors who normally bought and sold bonds routinely froze in their tracks, fearing that any firm with which they traded might be hiding big losses and would no longer be a viable trading partner.

By late September, the Federal Reserve, led by New York Fed president William McDonough, convinced a consortium of private institutions, which included Merrill Lynch and Goldman Sachs, to take over LTCM and rescue the ailing firm.

Additionally, the Fed, led by its chairman, Alan Greenspan, cut interest rates to ease the cash crunch that was building on Wall Street. In the autumn of 1998, the Fed cut rates three times, once again saving the system from itself and from investors' failure to heed the message of the markets. The Fed's rapid rate-cutting action spurred a new bull market on Wall Street, driving the Dow from a low of nearly 7500 on October 8 to a series of new all-time highs that, by January 14, 2000, exceeded 11,700.

Crises often have unintended but positive results. They also frequently speed the process of reform, be it political, economic, or social. Sometimes, the economic changes are epochal and immediately apparent. In still other instances, crises speed along a process that is essential to change.

Such was the case in the late 1990s, when the financial market calamities that dotted the latter half of the decade encouraged all countries to expand the global trading system and to attempt, anyway, to establish a rules-based trading regime that would include all countries big and small.

President Bill Clinton made an enormous pitch at the end of his second term to get China into the family of nations, at least economically. His intense efforts to include China in the World Trade Organization (WTO) faced an uphill battle. But the attempt was seen as a move to keep China from becoming a future economic or political problem by making it part of the solution.

In one rare instance, Wall Street failed to anticipate an important moment in United States–China relations. Having been burned by the failure of the Clinton Administration to secure a deal in April of 1999, Wall Street reacted warily to subsequent efforts later that year. But when the administration announced a surprise agreement in November of 1999, the market *reacted* dramatically. The following story is a telling example of how market *reactions* are far less helpful in predicting the future than purely *anticipatory* moves. When the markets actually *know* something, they move before the event. If they are taken by surprise, they move after the event. It is imperative that one recognize and understand the difference.

In November of 1999, a reactive move in the stock market sent a message to the world, but the message was as questionable as the event itself.

China Fun

On November 15, 1999, the United States and China signed a historic trade agreement designed to bring the People's Republic into the World Trade Organization. It was a massive accord that is expected to open China's market of 1.2 billion people to American companies eager to do business along the old Silk Road.

In a fascinating display of euphoria, shares of Chinese companies that might one day benefit from this market-opening measure rallied fiercely around the time of the agreement. The stock market attempted, in this instance rather feebly, to anticipate how the new deal would affect trade between two of the most important nations in the world.

The story of these Chinese stocks underscores how the market can sometimes be blindsided by events, rather than anticipate them. But as the charts will illustrate, it is often quite clear when investors are engaging in simple guesswork about the future and when they actually know, in advance, the outcome of an uncertain situation.

In April of 1999, President Clinton, meeting with China's premier, Zhu Rongji, reportedly put his arm around the reform-minded leader and told him it was not politically possible for the Clinton administration to cut a trade deal with the Chinese. The president's pessimism was obvious despite the massive concessions China had offered the United States to conclude a sweeping bilateral agreement. The United States and China had struggled for months, if not years, over reaching an accord that would open up trade between the two countries and simultaneously allow China to enter the World Trade Organization, the 138-member country club that sets the rules for international commerce.

The United States had worked diligently to open China's potentially vast markets in agriculture, financial services, telecommunications, and media. China, for its part, wanted the prestige of being part of the world economic community while also gaining normal trade relations with the United States, rather than face an annual Congressional vote over whether China should be allowed most-favored-nation status.

In April, a Republican-controlled, and still restive, U.S. Congress, reeling from its inability to drive Bill Clinton from office, made it quite clear it would not approve the president's planned trade deal with Beijing. The president relayed this to Premier Zhu, who dejectedly headed back to China without a deal and facing some enormous political risks of his own back home.

But in November, all of that changed. The U.S. trade representative, Charlene Barshefsky, and Gene Sperling, the president's top economic advisor, concluded a trade accord with Beijing. Shares of companies doing business in or with China went on an intercontinental ballistic tear. China Prosperity Holdings, a small, Hong Kong–based firm specializing in real estate, exploded from about 50¢ per share a few days before the deal was announced to $80 per share when word hit the street.

Investors irrationally assumed that any stock that had the word *China* in it would benefit immediately from broadening economic partnership between Washington and Beijing. They were simply guessing or playing the lottery. Shares of China Prosperity crashed within a matter of months, because the deal had yet to be approved by Congress in early 2000.

In the space of days, investors assumed that the trade accord, which *will likely* improve economic relations between East and West, would have an immediate and positive bottom-line influence on many, many companies that trade in the U.S. markets. Only time will tell if they are right. But the immediate message was that the world changed dramatically on November 15, 1999, and that the new world order was being defined by the action in the financial markets.

CHINA PROSPERITY—NOVEMBER 1999–FEBRUARY 2000.

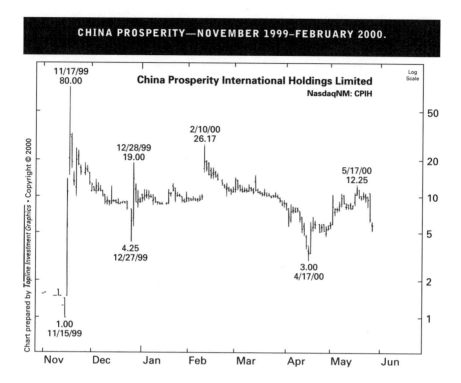

China Prosperity International Holdings Limited
NasdaqNM: CPIH

Chart prepared by *Topline Investment Graphics* • Copyright © 2000

11/17/99
80.00

12/28/99
19.00

2/10/00
26.17

5/17/00
12.25

4.25
12/27/99

3.00
4/17/00

1.00
11/15/99

Log Scale

Many times the prices of stocks, bonds, and commodities accurately anticipate or forecast future events. There are also times, as we've seen in this instance, when investors *react* to events and make broad assumptions about impending change. It is usually the anticipatory moves that bear watching. The reactive moves rarely send a message worth heeding.

4

Both a Borrower and a Lender Be

Misquoting Shakespeare is not my stock-in-trade, but for the purposes of this book, it is best to remember that the immortal bard was not always right. In the modern world, much unlike Hamlet's Denmark, responsible citizens often borrow and lend money to manage their daily affairs. Credit is the lifeblood of today's economy, and while its use and abuse can be dangerous to your financial well-being, credit plays an important role in securing your financial goals.

Nevertheless, that does not mean credit should be used unwisely or indiscriminately. Professional investors are intimately familiar with the long-time maxim of the moneyed class, "Borrow cheap but lend dear." Up until now, the general public had a tendency to do just the opposite. But with the advent of real-time financial information, the development of the Internet, and more sophisticated financial tools, it's becoming increasingly possible for individuals to act just as the moneyed classes always have.

In this chapter, we will examine the market messages that emanate from some key indicators—indicators that will help you decide when money is cheap or dear—indicators that will help you borrow or lend much more profitably.

Consumers in the United States borrow hundreds of billions of dollars a year. They borrow to purchase homes, cars, appliances, computers, and the myriad other products and services that make life more livable. But wouldn't it be wonderful if the average consumer could get the best rate on every loan as often as possible?

If you pay attention to the message of the credit markets, you can do just that. In this chapter we'll show you key financial market indicators that reveal just which way interest rates are heading and how you can use a companion Internet site on CNBC.com to get a daily read on the interest rate outlook. When taken in concert, these market indicators will make you as savvy at forecasting interest rates as some of Wall Street's most renowned "Fed watchers!"

Remember, the cost of money is the single most important component of any financial equation, from the long-term direction of the stock market to the ultimate cost of your very own home. There is no more important financial issue on either Wall Street or Main Street. It's time to look at borrowing and lending in exactly the same way as the pros always have.

Utility Value

Nineteen ninety-four was the second worst year in the bond market since 1927. It wasn't just that interest rates went up at the most precipitous pace since the Roaring Twenties. The real problem was that almost no one saw it coming—despite some important market indicators that were clearly flashing major warning signals. Utility stocks, as an important example, have the power to forecast the direction of interest rates. Despite their solid track record in identi-

---

NOTE: The Message of the Markets web site at CNBC.com will prove useful here, as well. We've assembled a group of indicators (about which you are going to read more in the following pages) that will give you a comprehensive look at where interest rates are heading in both the short and the long term. When taken in sum, these amazingly sensitive interest rate indicators will help you make extremely informed borrowing decisions. In addition to helping you buy a home, lock in a mortgage, or refinance outstanding debt, our key "rate watch" segment will also allow you to make better bets on the financial markets.

fying changes in rates, many people choose to ignore this indicator. It's hard to know why.

Although Main Street barely felt the impact of rising interest rates in 1994, Wall Street was decimated by the unexpected rise in the cost of money. The carnage was severe. Entire brokerage firms went bust. Hedge funds, sophisticated money management firms, disappeared, and in some cases, literally overnight. Mutual funds, thought to be safe by the investing public, suffered severe and surprising losses that threatened the health of that booming business, if only for a brief period of time. An entire county in Southern California declared bankruptcy as a consequence of the bond market's brutal year.

The entire story of the bond market's collapse was foretold by one key stock market average, well in advance of the credit market crisis. The Dow Jones Utility Average, one of the stock market's most sensitive interest rate gauges, flashed a bright red stoplight in the autumn of 1993. No one on Main Street and, surprisingly, no one on Wall Street ever noticed.

Many average Americans probably don't recall the turbulence that occurred in the financial markets in 1994. In fact, for many on Main Street, 1994 was just another year in which the economy grew at an acceptable pace, many new jobs were created, and the memories of a recent recession began to dim.

But on Wall Street it was quite a different story: 1994 was a bloodbath.

Until that fateful year, Wall Street firms were having something of a party—a money printing party. For the previous three years the Federal Reserve had kept interest rates quite low, allowing big banks and brokerage firms to borrow cheaply and invest profitably in an environment where both stocks and bonds rallied in nearly a straight line toward heaven. The Dow Industrial Average jumped from nearly 3000 in 1991 to nearly 4000 in early 1994: a quite respectable performance by the standards of the day. Bond market interest rates dropped precipitously in those years, greatly increasing the value of existing, higher-yielding bonds.

Suddenly, in early 1994, all of that changed. The Federal Reserve, fearing an overheating economy on Main Street and a dangerously speculative episode on Wall Street, began raising interest rates to cool down both sectors of the economy. The Fed raised interest rates seven times in a little over a year, pushing short-term interest rates from 3 percent all the way to 6 percent, a stunning doubling in rates that hurt anyone whose business depended on the constant flow of easy money.

Wall Street was taken by surprise. The sudden shift in rates meant that using borrowed money to buy stocks and bonds wouldn't necessarily result in easy profits, as it had in the past. It also meant that some firms, who had used cheap, borrowed money to speculate in some highly complex, interest-sensitive investments, were about to see their fortunes change, significantly, for the worse.

One of Wall Street's hottest hedge funds of the early 1990s was a firm known as Granite Askin. Run by a *wunderkind* in the mortgage securities market, David Askin, the firm imploded overnight when its highly leveraged portfolio of mortgage bonds shriveled up. His brokerage house partners liquidated the portfolio in a day, wiping out $600 million of investment capital in an instant.

Even mutual funds were not immune to the sudden shift in interest rates. Some presumably "plain vanilla" mutual funds, and the presumably riskless money market funds, ran into trouble after they, too, speculated in risky interest-sensitive securities.

But the greatest debacle of all occurred in a most unlikely place, the conservative enclave known as Orange County, California.

Orange County, for decades, was a fast-growing collection of hamlets that prospered as the Southern California economy boomed in the 1970s and 1980s. Home to many defense firms, savings and loan institutions, banks, real estate operations, and massive shopping malls, Orange County had a history of solid growth, rising real estate values and, of course, beautiful weather. It was a paradise for many baby boomers who wanted the fast pace of Los Angeles living, without the congestion and aggression of its sister county to the north.

Orange County's urban sprawl was more controlled and better

planned than that of other fast-growing communities. Its chiefly conservative local officials were fiscally prudent and morally sound, or so it appeared prior to December 1994, when that belief would be severely shaken as Orange County plunged into the chaos that had overcome the nation's credit markets.

In late December 1994 rumors began to swirl on Wall Street that a major brokerage house, Merrill Lynch, was having some sort of financial trouble related to its relationship with a U.S. municipality. The rumors were vague and unclear. The relationship was sketchy, at best. But in a matter of hours, it became increasingly clear to financial reporters, like myself, that Orange County, California, was in the midst of a major financial crisis that mushroomed as interest rates headed higher and higher on faraway Wall Street.

To put it as simply as possible, Orange County's treasurer, Robert Citron, a seemingly unassuming and somewhat unsophisticated character, used billions of dollars of borrowed money to speculate in complex investments known as derivatives. These often misunderstood securities had strange names like *reverse repurchase agreements, inverse floaters,* and *principal-only strips.* And these derivatives were highly sensitive to fluctuations in interest rates, particularly the sudden shift in rates that took place in 1994.

Citron's big bets, which leveraged the county's $2-billion cash hoard into a $20-billion portfolio of speculative investments, went bust in December as the persistent and precipitous rise in rates was nearing its peak. The portfolio plunged in value as Citron's reverse repurchase agreements went bust. (Reverse repurchase agreements increase in value as interest rates fall.)

The county lost $2 billion, putting its entire cash position in jeopardy. Citron's speculative portfolio was liquidated at a loss. The Orange County municipal government was thrown into total disarray. Planned projects were postponed or cancelled for lack of funds. Taxes were raised. County officials were booted from office and Robert Citron went to jail.

All of this carnage could have been easily avoided, or certainly greatly minimized, had market participants paid attention to some key market indicators that warned of an impending jump in interest rates.

Consider, for instance, the behavior of the Dow Jones Utility Average, a collection of 20 utility company stocks that tracks the performance of the electric utility and natural gas businesses. Utility companies are very sensitive to changes in interest rates since big power firms use lots of borrowed money to finance their ongoing operations. Because utilities are quite dependent on borrowed money to operate, they are also quite sensitive to even the smallest fluctuations in interest rates. The lower rates go, the more profitable the power companies can be, and vice versa.

So it's no surprise, then, that smart stock market investors use utility company stocks as a proxy for interest rates themselves. Indeed, throughout market history, the so-called smart money in the stock market has had an uncanny knack for buying utility stocks before interest rates fall, and selling them before interest rates rise. Such was the case in late 1993, when the Dow Jones Utility Average peaked and subsequently sold off more sharply than at any other time in recent memory.

On September 13, 1993, the Dow Utility Average hit an all-time high of 221.51. But the rally stopped dead in its tracks that very day. The smart money, sensing a coming shift in rates, began selling utility company shares with a vengeance. It was a sell-off that would ultimately drive that average down more than 30 percent by the middle of the following year. It would also presage the worst bear market in bonds in over half a century.

As the chart shows, the predictive power of utility stocks is quite phenomenal. While utilities peaked on September 13, the price of the benchmark 30-year Treasury bond would peak one month later on October 15, with its yield falling to a near record low of 5.7 percent. It was the highest price and lowest yield the bond market had seen since before the great inflation battles of the 1970s and early 1980s.

Other interest-sensitive stocks also flashed warning signs. Big banks and big brokerage houses that rely on borrowed money to finance their operations also weakened just before bond prices peaked

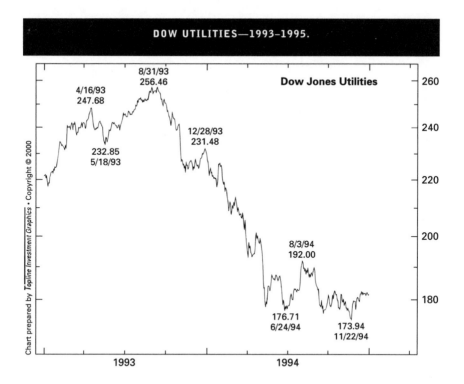

and interest rates bottomed out. In both instances, interest-sensitive stocks gave clear and relatively precise signals that rates were indeed about to rise. But as the previous stories amply illustrate, few money managers and other interested parties who were equally sensitive to changes in the cost of money bothered to heed the market's call.

It was a costly mistake that could have been avoided. Just ask Robert Citron.

Interestingly enough, many of those same interest-sensitive indicators were flashing warning signals at the end of 1999. The Dow Jones Utility Average was one of a few market indexes actually down for the year. In 1999, the bond market suffered its worst year since the Treasury began issuing bonds and tracking their performances in 1927. The total return on the Treasury's benchmark 30-year bond was minus 13 percent!

As always, key financial market indicators foretold of 1999's costly interest rate environment. Electric utility stocks flashed

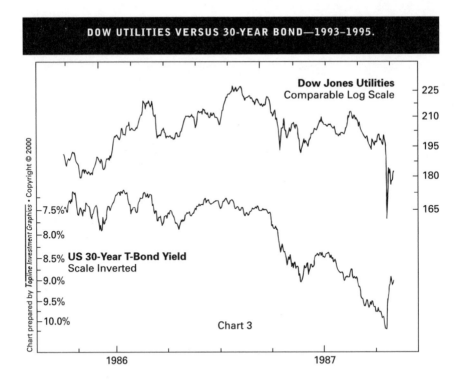

important warnings as did bank stocks and corporate borrowing habits. We'll examine more indicators shortly, but first a look at the most important credit market indicator of all, one that occurs as a result of rising interest rates. It is an indicator of great importance to everyone and can tell you, with a great degree of accuracy, whether rising interest rates will lead to a recession in less than a year. It's an important message-sending mechanism that everyone should consider.

The Yield Curve

There's an old joke in the economics profession. What's the difference between a recession and a depression? In a recession, your neighbor loses his job. In a depression, you do.

Wouldn't it be nice if everyone had ample warning of a recession? Not only to avoid losing one's job but also to prepare adequately for leaner times? There is a way to do that, if one pays close attention to a little-known bond market indicator known as the *yield curve.*

The yield curve sounds fairly arcane, but in reality the concept of how to interpret it, is quite simple. The yield curve measures the relationship of short-term interest rates to long-term interest rates. Short-term rates are generally lower than long-term rates because investors demand a higher rate of return (or interest rate) when they lend money for longer periods of time. The longer the term of the loan, the higher the rate of interest paid by the borrower. The reason for that has to do with risk. The longer one's money is tied up in the bond market, the more the lender's principal is at risk of being devalued by an unexpected economic event, particularly inflation.

Inflation eats away at one's investments and makes the investment principal worth less and less over time. So investors demand that borrowers compensate them for that risk by paying higher rates of interest.

The U.S. government, for instance, borrows money from the public all the time. It does so by issuing T-bills, T-notes, and T-bonds. T-bills are debt instruments that mature in 3 months, 6 months, or 1 year. T-notes mature in 2 to 10 years while T-bonds mature in 20 or 30 years. Under normal economic circumstances, T-bills may yield 4 percent. T-notes may yield 5 percent and T-bonds may yield 6 percent. The yield curve looks at the upward slope of interest rates from 3-month T-bills to the 30-year bond. That curve slopes gently higher in normal times. Investors get a little interest for lending money for 3 months and they get a considerable amount more for lending money for 30 years.

An upward slope in the yield curve implies to economists (and more importantly to the Federal Reserve) that investors expect few disruptive events in the near term and gently rising inflation over the next 30 years. When the yield curve steepens dramatically, however, investors are demanding higher and higher rates of interest

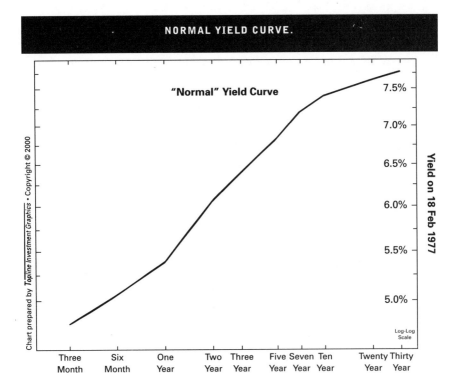

NORMAL YIELD CURVE.

"Normal" Yield Curve

7.5%

7.0%

6.5%

6.0%

5.5%

5.0%

Yield on 18 Feb 1977

Chart prepared by *Topline Investment Graphics* · Copyright © 2000

Log-Log
Scale

| Three Month | Six Month | One Year | Two Year | Three Year | Five Year | Seven Year | Ten Year | Twenty Year | Thirty Year |

because they are growing increasingly uncertain about the long-term future. They want higher rates as compensation for the risk they assume when lending money for 30 years.

The message of a very steep yield curve could be that inflation is likely to accelerate to damaging levels sometime in the life of that investment. (Inflation is the archenemy of bond investors. Inflation eats into the principal investment, cutting the purchasing power of the return on bonds.) A so-called steep yield curve sends a message to investors that interest rates may have to rise in order to slow economic growth and nip any incipient inflationary pressures in the bud.

Indeed, when those conditions occur, the Federal Reserve does raise interest rates to cool an overheating economy, a phenomenon investors witnessed and, to an extent, suffered through in 1999. Once in a great while, the Fed raises short-term interest rates so dramatically that they rise faster than long-term interest rates. That process leads to a curious development along the yield curve. The yield curve may actually "invert," where short-term rates rise above long-term interest rates. That inverted yield curve has ominous implications for the economy.

A recent study by the New York Federal Reserve has shown that an inverted yield curve is the most accurate, single predictor of a coming recession. The yield curve inverts because the Federal Reserve is rapidly raising rates to slow down the economy and beat back the threat of inflation. At some point in that process, however, the rate rise is so steep and so punishing to economic growth, choking off demand for business loans, mortgages, and other forms of credit, that growth stops dead in its tracks. At that point, bond investors suddenly realize that with growth slowing, or disappearing altogether, inflation will not become a problem and will no longer hurt their bond investments. It is then that investors begin purchasing bonds. And as bond prices rise, yields on those long-term treasury securities fall, even as the Fed is still raising rates. In other words, the yield curve described previously inverts.

Bond investors, essentially then, are betting that a recession, induced by rising interest rates, will make their bond holdings more valuable. Invariably, the inversion of the yield curve is the most potent market signal that a recession is just around the corner. The New York Federal Reserve shows that in a period in which the yield on 2-year Treasury notes exceeds 30-year bond yields for a period of several months, a recession is a virtual certainty within 9 to 12 months.

The data are incontrovertible. There is no other simple indicator that can so persuasively provide important economic information upon which one can act.

The implications of an inverted yield curve can be quite serious. As we all know, recessions are painful economic periods for most people. The period just before a recession, when interest rates are going up, hurts individuals and companies that have borrowed excessively in the recent past. As their respective interest burdens rise, corporate and household cash flow shrinks, causing retrenchment and, often, bankruptcies.

In recessions, corporations cut back and people lose their jobs. Those who have not saved for rainy days may suffer serious setbacks when their jobs, seemingly without adequate notice, disappear. *Without notice* is a key concept here. Recessions never come from out of the blue. There are always multiple warning signs, and in the case of an inverted yield curve, one very clear sign that there's danger ahead.

Similarly, economists note that when the inversion ends, and the yield curve begins to steepen again, a recovery is just around the corner. At that stage of the cycle a steepening of the yield curve does not forecast inflation, but renewed growth. Economists also note that as the yield curve steepens, it is a great time to buy bonds.

It is impossible to stress too much how important an early warning signal for recession can be. Imagine if you knew that a recession was a near certainty in 9 to 12 months. Would you spend less and save more for a rainy day?

Would you examine your job, your industry, your level of train-

---

NOTE: There have been two periods in the last several years during which the yield curve appeared to invert. One came in the summer of 1998, when the collapse of Long-Term Capital Management and Russia's financial troubles caused global investors to purchase mass quantities of U.S. Treasury bonds as a hedge against worldwide economic calamity. The net effect of those purchased was to drive down long-term interest rates so much that they fell below short-term interest rates. The yield curve inverted but it wasn't because short rates were rising more quickly than long rates. Hence a recession was not indicated.

In late 1999 and early 2000, the yield curve began to invert as the Federal Reserve raised short-term rates. But the inversion was exacerbated by a government plan to buy back billions of U.S. Treasury bonds with the federal government's bulging budget surplus. The yield curve inversion, again, was not a clear indicator of future economic trends. Its message was muddled by unusual and unexpected circumstances. By the time this book is printed, we will know whether or not the yield curve inversion of the year 2000 was a recession warning or just a false alarm.

Recession warnings have their roots in rising interest rates. Now let's examine some of the most important indicators that can tell you, quite precisely, which way interest rates are headed. These indicators will help you time your home purchases or help you lock in a more favorable mortgage rate. They can also help you decide how you'd like to play the stock market. Will you sell a bank stock when interest rates are getting ready to fall? Doubtful. But will you buy a mortgage lender's stock when rates are about to rise? Probably not. The following indicators will prove essential to your financial future, provided you listen closely.

ing or education, in an effort to insulate yourself from potential employment problems?

Would you more rapidly pay down your mortgage, eliminate credit card debt, or refinance existing obligations to bolster your cash flow?

Professionals do all those things when they become convinced a problem is looming on the economic horizon. So should you.

Being Alan Greenspan

While utility stocks are quite useful in predicting both tops and bottoms in interest rate cycles and the longer term direction of rates as well, they don't tell investors much about when the Federal Reserve will raise or lower rates. There is, however, one key indicator that forecasts the Fed's moves with great precision. It's called the Fed Funds futures contract.

The Federal Funds rate is a key interest rate that the Federal Reserve uses to set monetary policy. In other words, it's a rate that the Fed uses to dictate the cost of money to banks, borrowers, and investors. The Fed Funds rate itself is the rate banks charge each other for overnight loans. (Banks often have to borrow money from one another on a short-term basis in order to square their books at the end of each banking day.) The Fed Funds rate is the shortest-term lending rate in the United States. In the 1990s, the Fed Funds rate has been as low as 3 percent and as high as 6 percent, though it has traded both higher and lower in past decades.

When the Fed sets that rate for banks, it essentially sets lending rates for everyone, since banks base their own loan rates on Fed Funds. The Federal Reserve has used other lending rates to set monetary policy in the past, but for the purposes of this discussion, we will assume that the Fed Funds rate is the rate the Fed will target in the future to signal its policy intentions.

As always, Wall Street has been able to develop a futures contract based on the Federal Funds rate. That contract trades on the Chicago Board of Trade and is used as a proxy for the true Fed

Funds rate charged by banks. Bond traders buy and sell Fed Fund futures based on their perceptions of what the Fed is likely to do with interest rates when it meets in Washington.

The Federal Reserve's policymaking body, the Federal Open Markets Committee, assembles every six weeks to review economic conditions in the United States and decide whether interest rates need to be raised or lowered, as conditions dictate. (As we have pointed out in previous chapters, the Fed's main goal is to have the U.S. economy grow as quickly as possible without generating inflation, a damaging economic problem that robs all citizens of their purchasing power.)

Investors with knowledge of the Fed's frequently mysterious ways make bets on Fed policy by buying and selling Fed Fund futures. As Fed Funds rise in value, investors are betting the Fed will likely leave rates alone, or even lower them. As Fed Funds fall, investors are betting the Fed will likely raise rates at its next policy meeting.

Analyst Jim Bianco, a financial market historian, has been studying the behavior of Fed Fund futures for quite some time and has found that they are startlingly accurate when predicting just what the Fed will do. Since 1994, Fed Fund futures, through their price action, have presciently forecast the Fed's decision on interest rates 39 times. Its accuracy rate is above 80 percent! Very few financial indicators can boast that degree of precision in predicting the future. What's even more amazing about the predictive value of Fed Fund futures is that they are most accurate between 10 and 13 days before a scheduled Fed meeting, as the table illustrates.

The tricky part about using Fed Fund futures to estimate the chances of the Fed raising or lowering interest rates is that it does require the interested party to do a little math homework. (Images of late night struggles with algebra and trigonometry immediately spring to mind, causing one's forehead to break out into a cold sweat.)

Cold sweats aside, I will quote Jim Bianco's work to ensure that

I accurately convey the process by which one can use this observation to predict what the Fed will do to the cost of money.

> The Fed Funds futures contract is a monthly average of the effective Fed Funds rate (not the actual target rate itself). Over an entire month, however, the effective rate and the target rate are almost identical.
>
> So, if you assume that the Fed Funds rate holds at 5.25 percent through October 5, (for example) and then moves to 5.50 percent for the rest of the month, it will average 5.46 percent for the month of October. (November is the contract month that is used to predict the Fed's action in the month of October.) The difference between the effective rate and the average is 21 basis points. (That's about a fifth of a percentage point.)
>
> After figuring out that difference, one takes the implied Fed Funds rate found in the closing price of the futures contract, which for the purposes of this discussion was 5.285 percent. Subtract the targeted rate (5.25 percent) from the implied rate.
>
> The difference there is 3.5 basis points. Divide 3.5 into 21 (from the previous calculation). The result is 16.66 percent. In other words, on that particular day on which the calculation was made, the November [1999] Fed Fund futures contract was predicting only a 16.6 percent chance that the Fed would raise rates at its October 5 meeting.

All the data required for the calculation are available in the *Wall Street Journal,* on CNBC.com, or from a variety of other sources. Or you may wish to watch CNBC, which generally discusses this topic on a frequent basis in the weeks leading up to a Fed decision on interest rates, making it easy for the layperson to assess the chances that rates will go either up or down.

In late 1999, this indicator had one of its wildest rides ever. But the wild gyrations proved the immense usefulness of the Fed Funds contract as a tool for forecasting Fed policy. Despite some wild twists and turns in the days leading up to the Fed's decision on interest rates on November 16, the contract proved deadly accurate once again. By October 1999, the Federal Reserve, citing tight labor markets and potential inflationary pressures, had raised interest rates twice in four months, attempting to rein in the fast-growing economy and keep a lid on inflation. The Fed had, in essence, taken back two of the three rate cuts it undertook in the fall of 1998, when it was combating the potentially ill effects of the global economic crisis.

But by late October 1999, investors, analysts, and economists were split over whether the Fed would hike rates again in November. Investors, in particular, fear three consecutive rate hikes by the Fed since, historically, three interest rate increases have led to bear markets on Wall Street many, many times. By mid-2000, the Fed had raised rates a few more times hoping to slow the pace of a breakneck economic recovery that threatened to reignite inflationary pressures in the United States.

A brief digression here. In the 1970s, a stock market analyst, Edson Gould, was a pioneer in technical analysis of the stock market. Technical analysts use charts and other quantitative data to predict the direction of the stock market, using price histories, valuation benchmarks, and other tools in an effort to forecast what's next on Wall Street. Mr. Gould discovered, through his careful research, that every time the Federal Reserve raised its discount rate (a key short-term lending rate) three times in a row, the stock market slumped. He dubbed his finding the "three steps and a stumble" rule. And indeed, market history shows that on nearly all occasions in this century, three rate hikes usher in a bear market in stocks. (A bear market is defined as a 20 percent decline in the market averages from their most recent highs.)

So you can see why, in the autumn of 1999, investors were so preoccupied with the Fed's impending decision on interest rates. A November hike could trigger the "three steps and a stumble" rule, possibly bringing the greatest bull market of the post–World War II years to a sudden end. The Fed Funds futures contract let investors know exactly what to expect.

According to Jim Bianco, the contract was flashing a huge warning sign of a coming rate hike on October 29, 1999. Some 12 days before the Fed was scheduled to meet, the Fed Funds (FF) futures contract was predicting a 72 percent chance of a rate hike on November 16. Remember the FF futures contract has its greatest predictive power roughly 12 to 13 business days before the Fed makes it decision.

But only days before the FF futures flashed a warning, a curious thing occurred. Federal Reserve Board Chairman Alan Greenspan, speaking to members of the securities industry in Boca Raton, Florida, gave a speech that dramatically changed Wall Street's view of what the Fed was likely to do with interest rates a few weeks hence. Mr. Greenspan, referencing the inflation-fighting prowess of the modern, high-tech economy, appeared to some observers to be saying that inflation was not a current economic problem and that there was no need for the Fed to raise rates further. (That was the interpretation, not the reality.)

A day or so later, after mulling the contents of Mr. Greenspan's speech, investors decided a rate hike was not likely. With the help of some "friendly" economic data that showed the inflation threat to be retreating, Fed Funds suddenly shifted dramatically. By November 5, the odds for a rate hike had plummeted to only 42 percent.

But once again, the prevailing winds shifted as a confusing piece of economic news was released on Wednesday, November 10. Inflation at the wholesale level actually declined by one-tenth of 1 percent. That was viewed as great news. But another key measure of wholesale inflation, the so-called core inflation rate (which excludes unpredictable food and energy costs), rose a greater-than-expected three-tenths of 1 percent. That number implied that inflationary pressures were still building, contrary to other recent reports. The Fed Funds futures contract suddenly shifted again so that by the end of the day, the odds for a rate hike had jumped back to 58 percent.

From that day until the Fed actually raised rates, the contract showed with increasing certainty just what the Fed would do.

On Friday, November 12, the odds jumped to 62 percent.

By Monday, November 15, the odds rose to 76 percent.

With one hour to go before the Fed announced that it was raising rates, the Fed Funds futures contract suggested that there was an 88 percent chance of a rate hike, even as policymakers met in a closed-door session in Washington, D.C.

By Jim Bianco's measure, the FF contract, which he had been following closely for two years, correctly predicted the outcome of 24 consecutive meetings. No economist or avowed Fed watcher could boast of such a successful track record in predicting the Fed's decision on interest rates.

Bianco notes that it is quite surprising that the contract has such impressive predictive powers. On average, only about 11,000 Fed Fund futures contracts are traded daily. That pales in comparison with the hundreds of thousands of bond futures contracts that change hands every day at the Chicago Board of Trade. The contract, he says, is ripe for manipulation, since it is so thinly traded. But so far, that has not been an issue.

The integrity of the action in the FF contract remains intact.

Jim Bianco noticed in late 1999 that the contract enjoys its peak predictive power 13 business days before the Fed meets to decide the cost of money. Interestingly, he observed that on two occasions in 1999, veteran *Washington Post* correspondent John Berry had written articles about the Fed's intentions exactly 13 days before Fed policymakers gathered in the Fed's executive conference room. Berry, who covers the Federal Reserve for the *Post,* is regarded as one of the best-connected Fed watchers in business journalism. Citing "unnamed Fed sources," Berry is rarely wrong about how the Fed is likely to act when it holds an interest rate meeting.

Bianco is not a conspiracy theorist and doesn't believe that two reports make a trend. But he is now also watching the news flow in the days leading up to a Fed meeting to see if there are any discernable patterns of selective disclosure that might also be helpful to investors in the years ahead.

Professional investors watch this indicator quite closely. They believe that having access to an accurate forecasting tool that tells them if and when interest rates will go up helps them make wise investing and consuming decisions. For the individual investor, advance knowledge of the Fed's actions is hard to come by. This indicator gives that advance warning that can help an individual time his or her stock market investments or lock in a mortgage, or even decide when to pay down debt or prepay a home equity line of credit. The cost of money is a key variable in our economic lives. Knowing whether that cost is going up or down is an important thing, for professionals and individuals alike.

Jim Bianco recommends heeding the message of the Fed Fund futures market if *you'd* like an advance warning of what the Fed will do.

Financial professionals use market messages like the one previously discussed to time their own borrowing and lending practices. Some big companies have become quite astute in making a decision about when to borrow money. No company has proved more adept than IBM.

We now listen to yet another market message that can help you make better, more profitable moves in the financial world. And when a company this big sends a message, you'd better listen!

When Big Blue Borrows . . .

The goal of this exercise is to borrow money like a professional on Wall Street. Whether your goal is to save yourself money on a mortgage or refinance an existing loan, the markets can tell you when to act and when to act *quickly!*

For most Americans the largest single purchase they will ever make is a home. It is the largest single monthly expense and, usually, the biggest debt ever incurred in one's lifetime. Yet, most people allow emotions and a host of other factors to influence the timing of a most important purchase. And while that is completely understandable, given the nature of the home buying experience, there are messages from the market that, at the very least, will help you get the least-expensive mortgage available.

The key is to act like a pro, coolly and rationally. Big corporations borrow money all the time. They borrow money to finance acquisitions, to pay down older, high-cost debt, or to help maintain cash flow as they wait for money to come in the door.

The corporate treasury department directs the borrowing activities for many companies. So the treasurer serves a very important function, acting as a key player in any company's financial future. It is often the treasurer who decides when to borrow money in the bond market. It is critical that he or she be extremely sensitive to coming changes in interest rates, so the company can borrow cheaply and use the proceeds profitably.

Nowhere in corporate America has the corporate treasurer been better at borrowing money than at International Business Machines, IBM.

IBM's borrowing habits are important to observe. Professionals pay very close attention to IBM. *Big Blue*, as it is known on Wall Street, can provide some very important clues about the direction of interest rates, particularly when interest rates are at the lows of a given cycle.

The world's biggest computer company has been more astute at borrowing money than many institutions that borrow and lend money for a living.

Indeed, many of the biggest corporations in the world have become quite adept at borrowing money on the cheap, locking in low rates of interest and using the proceeds to invest more profitably at higher rates of return. In 1999, hundreds of U.S. corporations borrowed money to lock in the cheapest interest rates available in over 20 years. In the first half of the year alone, over 4,000 companies borrowed $531 billion, the biggest corporate borrowing binge in several decades.

But why did these corporations go into hock in late 1998 and early 1999?

Let's take a look at recent market history.

In October of 1998 bond market interest rates plunged to just over 4.7 percent, the lowest yield on the Treasury's 30-year bond since the government began issuing those "long bonds" in 1977. The drop in rates was the by-product of a rout in the world financial markets touched off by an economic crisis in Russia and the collapse of a major East Coast hedge fund (investment fund) known as Long-Term Capital Management.

The financial crisis of that summer and autumn made all sorts of investments unattractive to well-heeled professionals. Their sudden aversion to risk in emerging markets, currencies, commodities, or even U.S. blue chip stocks sent them scurrying for cover into the world's safest investments, U.S. Treasury bills and bonds.

That rush into bonds sent interest rates plummeting in the United States to levels described a few paragraphs previous. The drop in rates, in turn, prompted a record number of Americans to refinance their homes, apply for new mortgages, buy cars, and finance all sorts of other activities with borrowed money. Corporations also took advantage of the precipitous drop in rates, borrowing money at a fast and furious pace.

The question, however, is how to determine when interest rates have seen their lows and are about to turn upward. That's where a study of professional borrowing is most profitable. Mimicking the pros allows individuals to lock in low rates just like corporate treasurers do.

The financial pages of the nation's major newspapers, the *Wall Street Journal*, and, of course, CNBC frequently discuss the borrowing habits of major corporations. They do so because corporate activity in the bond market has important implications for the direction of interest rates. The more heavy the corporate bond calendar, the greater the degree of corporate bond issuance, and the greater the chance that rates are going up, rather than down.

There is strength in numbers. When corporate treasurers see interest rates at multiyear or multidecade lows, they jump at the chance to borrow money, knowing full well that low interest rates are tantamount to a gift from God. Anyone with half a lifetime of experience borrowing money knows that interest rates can fluctuate wildly, as they did in the 1970s and 1980s. Bond market interest rates peaked in 1980 at 14 percent as inflation soared, oil prices skyrocketed, and gold vaulted to over $800 an ounce.

Individuals who borrowed money then paid dearly for the privilege. The prime lending rate, the rate that banks charged commercial customers, exploded to 20 percent! Rates have come down steadily as inflation declined to levels not seen since the 1960s.

You can see why it's important to borrow money cheaply. It can become quite dear in a relatively short space of time. IBM is quite successful at doing just that. Anytime IBM borrows money for 10 years or longer, by selling bonds, it has historically done so at the almost precise moment that interest rates are at their low point in that particular cycle. Consider the chart. In only one instance in the last 25 years has IBM failed to catch the exact low in rates when it issued 10-, 20-, 30-, or even 100-year bonds. That is a track record not to be trifled with!

If you had followed IBM's treasurer into the market and borrowed when he had, the cost savings on your mortgage could have been significant. Every time interest rates go up a half point, the cost of a $100,000 mortgage goes up by $33 per month or $396 per year. (That would increase the cost of a 30-year loan by $11,180—a 12 percent increase in the cost of the home. On a national basis, for every one point increase in mortgage rates, Americans pay an additional $250 billion in interest.)

NOTE: There is a fascinating footnote to the hectic pace of borrowing undertaken by U.S. corporations in the first half of 1999. Many companies borrowed heavily in the first and second quarters to avoid potential financial problems that may have been associated with the turn of the century. So-called Y2K concerns prompted some of the nation's largest firms, Ford, Wal-Mart, and others, to essentially line up all their financing for the remainder of the year in the event a financial panic ensued as a consequence of the turnover to the year 2000.

That was a message that individuals should have heard, as well. It pays to have one's financial house in order before, not during or after, an event that could have a significant impact on the economic landscape. Many of these firms saved significant sums of money by acting preemptively. By early 2000, interest rates were higher than they had been in several years. So the timely actions of these companies again illustrate quite clearly that markets and market participants always send signals that are useful to you.

But it's not just mortgage rates that are influenced by the cost of money. As we've said earlier, car loans, credit card rates, stock prices, and the economy are greatly influenced by interest rates. Knowing when rates are going to turn can be quite helpful in planning your immediate financial future.

That's why it pays to follow Big Blue.

5

The Real World

It is becoming clear that the market's signal-sending mechanism can be very potent. Time and time again, financial markets have shown that through the collective wisdom of their investors, they can convey, with near precision, how the future will turn out.

What is even more exciting about studying the markets is that they can often forecast future events outside the world of Wall Street. That, indeed, is a bold claim to make for the markets. While financial news has become an integral part of American life, it has even invaded where pop culture, financial news, and general news often intersect. Most people just don't realize it.

Market history is replete with examples of how markets knew of important events, even though the events themselves were not initially economic in nature. There are instances in which the markets flashed warning signs of impending war or how markets actually discounted the outcome of a military conflagration long before the general population perceived the tide to be turning. Certainly that was the case with the Gulf War (as it is commonly known) in 1991, when the oil markets sent strong signals about the coming catastrophe and its ultimate conclusion. You might be surprised to read in the next section that in one case the behavior of one oil and one textile stock accurately identified tensions between two Middle Eastern countries even before the politicos knew what was happening. In one other case, the price of wheat gave the world its first clue about the stunning magnitude of Chernobyl's nuclear accident back in 1986.

Sometimes, obscure sections of the financial markets send important signals about current events. By now, you probably are beginning to understand that markets do send important messages and accept the premise. In the next several sections, we hope to show how those messages can come from any market at any time, no matter how obscure or seemingly insignificant.

Professional investors, the best of them, are like market detectives. They follow clues wherever they lead in the fervent hope that those clues will provide important answers. The answers, in turn, they hope, will lead to important moneymaking opportunities.

The next stage of our process is to turn you into a savvy sleuth.

Enjoy the following detective stories.

Oil's Well That Ends Well

Does anyone recall the great controversy of the early 1990s relating to the Gulf War? There was, at the time, a searing debate about whether the U.S. diplomat in Baghdad had been warned of an impending strike against Kuwait by Saddam Hussein but then failed to pass along that critical intelligence to the White House. It seems a small matter now, but the failure of the intelligence community to anticipate Saddam's invasion caused quite a stir at the time.

Indeed, the U.S. ambassador to Iraq reportedly had been warned by Iraqi authorities that a strike against Kuwait was not only possible, but also likely. The ambassador went so far as to claim *publicly* that she had warned the White House that Saddam Hussein was threatening to invade its small but oil-rich neighbor. The White House then denied that such warnings were ever passed along. It was a messy exchange and an embarrassing one for President George Bush, who once ran the Central Intelligence Agency. For many Americans, Saddam Hussein's incursion into Kuwait was a total surprise.

But there were other warnings emanating from less "intelligent" quarters than Langley, Virginia. Those warnings came from an unlikely place—the world's financial markets. Had those warnings been heeded, it's altogether possible that the U.S. military machine could have anticipated and prevented the event, or at the very least, had more time to prepare for a potential conflict in the Middle East.

The price action in the world's crude oil markets was sending a distinct message in the late spring and early summer of 1990. But few people paid attention to an unexpected and unexplained rally in black gold. It was an attention lapse that would prove costly for the entire world.

Is it a surprise, in retrospect, that the U.S. intelligence community ignored strange goings on in the world's most important commodity market—the oil market? Particularly when the action in oil, the world's most important commodity, was so dramatic and yet inexplicable. Was it a surprise that the intelligence community failed to receive this important message?

The answer is a definitive yes.

In the spring of 1990, oil prices were remarkably well behaved. In fact, since 1986, when oil prices crashed to less than $10 per barrel, oil traded in a range between $10 and $18, keeping gasoline and other petroleum-based products quite affordable for American consumers. But as summer drew near in 1990, all that began to change.

Oil prices began to rise inexplicably in June of 1990. From a relatively low level of $16, the march toward $40 per barrel was stunning and brisk. Many analysts were quick to suggest that the increase in oil prices reflected market expectations that OPEC, the 13-member oil cartel, would engineer a price hike in midsummer by cutting back on oil production. The Organization of Petroleum Exporting Countries (OPEC), in its long and storied history, has often manipulated the market price of oil by alternately raising and lowering its output of petroleum. In some cases, like the Arab oil embargo in the early 1970s, OPEC's moves have devastating consequences for the world economy. At other times, OPEC's ability to raise or lower output has had a more subtle effect on the price of a barrel of crude.

OPEC tends to make these moves when prices are at extreme levels, cutting production when oil prices are in danger of collapsing to single digits and raising production when prices appear to have made oil too expensive for the world's gas-guzzling consumers.

At its summer meeting in July 1990, OPEC oil ministers decided to scale back oil production by a couple of million barrels per day to help firm up modestly slumping oil prices. This was a frequent game played by the cartel to keep oil prices firm. In some instances, OPEC need only say publicly that it planned a production cut to get oil prices moving higher. Every time OPEC drove the cost of oil down by producing too much crude, it made public statements that it would soon do just the opposite, promising to trim oil output in an effort to get prices back to a desired level. And, indeed, in late July 1990, the headlines carried the news from Vienna, "OPEC Oil Ministers Agree to Cut Daily Production."

The oil market, however, fully reflected that news by the time the ministers met in late July. The price of oil rose to a level that would reflect a couple-million-barrel reduction in supply long before the actual meeting took place, since the cartel gave plenty of warning about its July plans. (The oil market tends to anticipate events such as these by pricing in the well-telegraphed maneuvers of OPEC.)

Prices jumped from $16 to $25 per barrel in short order, an increase that more than fully reflected the anticipated reduction in crude oil supplies. There was, however, something of a problem in the oil market's behavior that summer. Prices kept going up—and fast.

The price of oil climbed inexorably through midsummer, leaving oil market traders, analysts, and even financial journalists scratching their heads. Why was the cost of the world's most important commodity still climbing? True, a reduction in oil output by the world's richest oil producing nations was an important event. But that event had been correctly anticipated by the market and was already priced in.

The continuing run-up in prices was unjustifiable relative to what the market knew of fundamental reality. There had to be

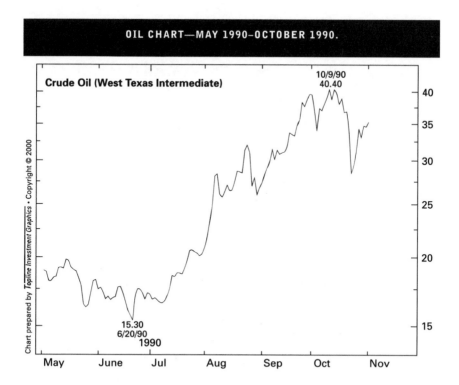

OIL CHART—MAY 1990–OCTOBER 1990.

Crude Oil (West Texas Intermediate)

10/9/90
40.40

15.30
6/20/90
1990

Chart prepared by *Topline Investment Graphics* • Copyright © 2000

another reason that prices kept rising. And that reason had to be important. It had to be big. And it had to suggest that the supply of crude oil might soon be disrupted.

In late July, the oil market was rife with vague rumors claiming that Iraqi troops were mobilizing somewhere near the Kuwaiti border.

Recall that at the time very few observers of Middle East politics or of oil market economics had publicly discussed even the remote possibility of another military excursion involving Iraq. Saddam Hussein's country was still reeling from an eight-year war with neighboring Iran. That conflagration cost Iraq a million lives and billions of dollars. Iraq seemed war-weary. It was nearly inconceivable that Saddam Hussein would soon embark on another potentially devastating campaign.

But the rumors lingered nonetheless. They grew more and more specific as the days passed until the final few days of the month.

At that point, the rumors became alarmingly specific. Iraqi troops *were* amassed on Kuwait's border. The border was imposed on the Iraqis by the British when they departed the Middle East in the mid-1900s. It was a border often questioned and finally challenged by the man known as the Butcher of Baghdad.

On August 2, 1990, Saddam Hussein invaded Kuwait. Oil prices exploded. In a matter of days, Kuwait's ruling al Sabah family had come under Saddam's rather oppressive thumb. Saddam not only controlled Iraq's oil producing capacity of four million barrels per day, but now also controlled Kuwait's output: two million barrels of oil daily. The prospects of reduced supplies from in and around the Persian Gulf region sent the oil markets into a mad panic. Prices raced to over $40 per barrel, higher than oil prices had ever gone before.

The spike in oil sent the cost of gasoline in the United States to its highest levels since the early 1980s. When combined with interest rates that had been rising since mid-1989, the one-two punch to the U.S. economy was too much for consumers to bear. The American economy was tipped into recession in late 1990. It was a recession that would ultimately knock the Gulf War's most noted hero, President George Bush, out of office.

But a more minute analysis of oil prices would show just how much the oil markets knew of the war's every twist and turn. Oil prices rallied for fully two months before Saddam Hussein's army set foot on Kuwaiti soil. Even more ironically, oil prices would see their peak two months before the Gulf War began, again illustrating the predictive powers of markets. The rally and subsequent crash in oil prices in early 1991 foretold all there was to tell about the Gulf War's surprising beginnings and equally surprising conclusion.

The key question remains: What did the oil market know and when did it know it? The answer? The market knew everything all along.

The rally in prices accurately foretold of a seminal event that would tip the world's supply-demand balance in a meaningful way. The crash in oil prices from October forward accurately predicted

Saddam Hussein's crushing defeat at the hands of the allied powers. Anthropomorphizing the financial markets to such an extent may be an exercise in folly. But a closer examination of the war's time line and the oil market's behavior shows a striking amount of forethought on the part of the smart money crowd in the oil arena.

Remember that movements in the prices of any market-traded goods reflect the cumulative wisdom of that market's participants. Remember also that some market participants trade on inside information, legal or not. They can profit handsomely from advance knowledge of market-moving events. If they know enough and have the financial resources to capitalize on that knowledge, the positions they take can influence the very markets in which they hope to make money. Those are the movements that are most meaningful and can be most helpful to other investors who are willing to pay attention to the message of the markets.

Pulitzer Prize–winning journalist Thomas L. Friedman of the *New York Times* has often speculated that Saddam Hussein trades oil futures in advance of his own market-moving activities. Indeed, Friedman once wrote that Saddam may have actually purchased oil futures in advance of some antagonistic military exercises that he staged just after the war, in an effort to whip up the oil market and generate some profits for himself (16). Desperately in need of hard currency thanks to the Allied embargo of Iraq, this was one way Saddam could earn a little income while banned from exporting oil into world's petroleum market.

Even though trading on inside information is illegal in the U.S. stock market, other financial markets around the world are not burdened by similar regulations and laws. Many a hedge fund speculator would admit privately that the world's currency and commodity markets are rife with trades made on inside information, for which there are few penalties, if any. And given Saddam Hussein's penchant for violating international conventions of all types, it is unlikely that insider trading would be something he finds particularly distasteful.

A complete deconstruction of the oil market's behavior between

May of 1990 and February of 1991 shows the market's uncanny ability to foretell every twist and turn in that bizarre series of events we called the Gulf War.

What was most striking about all market behavior, including oil, stocks, bonds, and currencies, was that on the very first day of the war they all behaved in a counterintuitive fashion. As hostilities broke out between the Gulf War allies and the forces of Saddam Hussein, every major market did exactly the opposite of what experts expected them to do.

Though it seems a distant memory now, political pundits and military analysts opined freely on American television that the allies would be facing a most formidable foe in Iraq's army. Despite their intense fatigue from the grueling, eight-year Iran-Iraq war, this battle-tested militia was the fourth-largest standing army in the world. Saddam's vaunted Republican Guard, Iraq's elite fighting force, was left virtually unscathed by the encounters with the Ayatollah Khomeini's army and was said to be up to any challenge posed by the West. As a consequence, many expected oil prices to skyrocket, interest rates to zoom higher, and stocks to crash.

But on January 17, 1991, a strange thing happened. Oil prices plunged. The Dow Jones Industrial Average gained a record 105 points. It was the largest point gain in market history. The U.S. dollar jumped in value. Gold fell in price. U.S. Treasury bonds, usually a repository of investor funds during times of uncertainty, declined in value as well.

Everything that happened in the markets that day was exactly the opposite of what experts expected. The breakout of hostilities was supposed to push oil prices back up. There were dire predictions at the time that a long, drawn out war would irreparably damage the oil producing capacity of Kuwait, Iraq, and maybe even Saudi Arabia—the world's largest oil exporter. There were very real fears that Saudi Arabia, which had allowed U.S. troops to stage their defense of Kuwait from Riyadh, would also be drawn into the conflict. A conflict on Saudi soil could cause a long-term interruption in the world's oil supply, the pundits proclaimed. Oil prices would skyrocket to $100 a barrel or more. The U.S. stock market would crash as a consequence of $100-a-barrel oil. As the stock market crashed, gold would hit $1000 per ounce. Interest rates would spike higher, the dollar would plunge, and the U.S. economy might even suffer a depression. That's what the experts worried about in the winter of 1991.

The markets knew better.

That worst case scenario never came to pass.

Maybe the markets took President Bush at his word, recalling that on August 5, 1990, the president, who was once derided as a "wimp," boldly declared that Iraq's invasion "will not stand" (17).

Maybe market participants were fully briefed on allied plans to remove Saddam Hussein from the Kuwaiti theatre. According to T.R. Fehrenbach's *This Kind of War,* U.S. military officials had "outlined a four-phased campaign ending with a ground offensive to drive Iraqi forces from Kuwait." The outlines of that campaign were drafted in October 1990, just as oil prices hit their highest level since the early 1980s. The plans for a major assault against Saddam's regime, though secret, were completed more than three months before the start of the war. Oil prices peaked as the plan was being finalized.

Whatever the case, the smart money truly knew something on January 17. It accurately anticipated the blistering assault the allies would launch against Iraq in Operation Desert Storm. The markets told the world that the West would win long before it was clear to military analysts, political pundits, or journalists.

The markets' behavior also reflected, quite presciently, the duration of the war, a mere 42 days. It culminated in a 100-hour ground war that led to a February 28 cease-fire. Saddam Hussein's "mother of all battles" would end in a brief but humiliating defeat.

The markets correctly ignored as minor Saddam Hussein's threats to attack Saudi Arabia, his scud-missile attacks on Israel, and his warnings of terrorist activities on American soil.

In short, the markets knew the war was over as soon as it began.

The greatest bull market to ever take place on Wall Street got its start on the day the Gulf War began. Now that was a message worth listening to.

Designer Jeans

The financial markets often can feel the winds of war, even when those winds ultimately fail to blow with full fury. The oil market clearly sent messages about Saddam Hussein's plans for Kuwait. But it was only the smart money crowd, possibly even Saddam Hussein himself, to whom the message of the market was apparent.

In the early 1980s, the stock market sent a signal of a war that wasn't to be. And again, only a few savvy traders on Wall Street were aware of the signs. Art Cashin, whom we met before, recently recalled in *Chronicles,* a Wall Street trade publication, some very strange market action one day some 20 years ago (18).

Cashin was competing with a veteran colleague on the floor of the New York Stock Exchange to bid on a certain stock. In the sometimes genteel society of floor brokers, rival brokers will often flip a coin to see who will bid first in a competitive trading situation. As the two combatants flipped for the privilege of executing a trade on behalf of their clients, Cashin noticed some rather unexpected action going on in oil and defense stocks.

International oil company shares began dropping while the shares of U.S.-based oil firms began to rise. Coincidentally, defense stocks also rallied in a manner that might attract some attention, even in the cynical world of Wall Street.

Cashin's competitor asked if he noticed the action in the oils.

As Art remembers it, he did his best Gary Cooper imitation, answering, "Yup," never willing to share too much information with a rival floor trader.

The broker intuitively opined, "Probably trouble in the Middle East."

Again, Cashin said, "Yup."

Despite obvious movement in these sensitive industries, the newswires had not yet reported anything that would explain the action in the stocks.

An hour or so later, Cashin's rival asked if he had been "watching the Oxy and the Indiana?"

Cashin said, "Yup," again, though he only said yup to avoid appearing ignorant.

The broker added, "The trouble is probably on the border between Egypt and Libya."

Cashin pondered the observation and agreed again. (By this time he wasn't sure why he was agreeing, but he figured it was best not to argue.)

It took Cashin a minute or two, but he eventually pieced together the logic his rival was using to deduce the exact location of this potential Middle East conflict.

Oxy, market slang for Occidental Petroleum, had a big presence in Libya. Indeed, its founder and then chief executive, Armand Hammer, had long-established ties with Moammar al Qaddafi and had been pumping oil in the rogue nation for decades.

Indiana, then called Standard Oil of Indiana, now called Amoco (recently merged with British Petroleum), was the biggest oil company in Egypt.

Both stocks were weakening without plausible explanation.

The news tickers on the floor made no mention of the situation.

After another hour passed by, the rival broker encountered Art again and asked if he had noticed the action in Cone Mills shares.

Cashin, growing a bit exasperated by the questions, blurted out to his inquisitor, "Why would I be watching a fabric company when war's about to break out?"

"Designer jeans," was his rival's only response.

"Sure!" Cashin said, as if the link was apparent to anyone but a fool.

The broker explained that Cone Mills, a major maker of designer jeans, had recently spent countless dollars refurbishing a cotton processing plant in northern Egypt.

In the early 1980s, designer jeans were still all the rage in New York. Cone Mills processed enormous amounts of Egyptian cotton, later shipping the processed cotton across the Mediterranean to Italy, where the jeans were made. After making the jeans and attaching fancy labels on the pants, the designer wear was shipped to the United States where anxious fashion mavens paid a few hundred dollars a pair for the privilege of looking good.

Cashin continued to explore his companion's logic on the floor. Cone Mills's weakness, along with the action in the oil stocks, suggested that the impending trouble in the Middle East would likely be located on the northern border of Egypt and Libya, where the Cone Mills processing plant was located. While the fortunes of the three companies seemed inextricably linked to two traders on the floor, the logic was refutable since the newswires made nary a mention of the Middle East for an entire day—until Art Cashin arrived at home.

As Cashin remembers that night, he arrived home, "turned on the TV news and on came one of the guys after Cronkite, but before Rather."

The top story as read by the anchor that night:

> Intelligence sources report that in order to avenge the assassination of (Egyptian) President Sadat, Hosni Mubarak of Egypt is massing troops along the border with Libya since Qaddafi is reported involved in the assassination.
>
> The same sources do not know if the potential invasion would come by land or sea, since the forces are massed near the northern or Mediterranean end of the border.

Cashin sat there amazed and vowed to start watching the action in Cone Mills more closely. And while the invasion never came, once again, the message of the market was clear.

Surprisingly, the market's ability to forecast is not limited to either financial or geopolitical events. Sometimes markets can tell us a great deal about an unfolding disaster that may have its roots in science or the environment. Market participants, investors, and short-term traders make their living ferreting out bits of information that give them a competitive edge in the marketplace. So when something important happens anywhere in the world, traders and investors frantically search for information that just might affect their investments.

Such was the case on an otherwise uneventful spring day in April 1986. The markets gave the first and most important signal of a developing environmental disaster. While the fallout from the market's behavior was ultimately and remarkably somewhat limited, the fallout from this disaster was not.

Chernobyl

What's 100 feet tall and has a beak and feathers?
Chicken Kiev.
How do you make Chicken Kiev?
Preheat your city to 10,000 degrees.

Wall Street traders have always been very adept at finding humor in even the most serious circumstances. This was true even in April 1986, when the world witnessed its most serious nuclear accident in history.

There was, of course, nothing funny about the incident, which killed thousands, injured more, and laid waste a large part of the Soviet Ukraine, the breadbasket of Russia.

But even more quickly than they made jokes about Chernobyl, traders in the financial markets reacted with lightning speed to just the slightest hint of trouble in a world far from home.

Many hours before the world knew what had happened on April 28, 1986, the wheat markets of Chicago were accurately forecasting some serious trouble in the growing region of the old Soviet Union. And while they were three days late in reacting to the actual event, the *American* wheat markets were the first markets to send a message that something was wrong. The most important aspect of this anecdote is that it illustrates that one can never know from which market an important message will emerge. That's why it's dangerous to ignore any unusual signals sent by a market—any market!

For no apparent reason, the price of wheat futures on the Chicago Board of Trade shot higher in the early morning of April 28. Commodity markets are known to be quite volatile. But in most instances, the volatility can easily be explained by the threat of drought, famine, flood, or news of an unexpected bumper crop. However, the action in the wheat market that morning was more notable than normal for its speed and for the nearly parabolic movement in the price of the grain.

Wheat is a most precious commodity in much of the world. Its price fluctuates from day to day, based on supply and demand, much like any other tradable commodity. Bumper crops in the heartland of America bring falling prices, while heavy demand from Asia, Europe, or India can drive prices higher on any given day.

Acts of God frequently have the most dramatic impact on the grain trade as droughts and floods alternatingly bring higher and lower prices for corn, wheat, and soybeans.

But in April 1986, the action in the grain markets was fairly stable. While a drought would ultimately drive grain prices higher later that summer, in the spring nature's fury was not yet news and, therefore, not yet an influence on agricultural commodities.

But there are acts of God and there are *acts of God!* The action that took place over a decade ago was more like the destruction of Sodom and Gomorrah than Noah's flood, as fire and brimstone rained down throughout Russia in the early spring of 1986.

Just after 1:20 A.M., on the morning of April 26, 1986:

[U]nit 4 of the Chernobyl nuclear power station experienced a surge in power from about .07 to some 100 times normal operating power. . . . The explosion blew off the top plate of the reactor exposing the core to air. This, in turn, gave rise to a hydrogen explosion a few seconds later and a subsequent graphite moderator fire. During this power surge, temperatures in the reactor core rose sufficiently to melt a significant portion [30 percent] of the enriched uranium fuel. This fuel subsequently beaded and was carried by the gases from the fire into the atmosphere. The prevalent winds at the time carried the radioactive debris northwest over Ukraine, Belorussia, Russia, Poland, Lithuania, Latvia, Estonia, Finland and Sweden (19).

This chilling account of Chernobyl's destruction, authored by the Ukrainian World Congress and reprinted by *Media Watch Ukraine,* graphically illustrates the size and scope of the explosion.

Ten years after the explosion, Professor David Marples of the University of Alberta, Canada, reported that the Chernobyl nuclear accident contaminated an area of 100,000 square miles in the Ukraine and Belorussia. Over 5700 cleanup workers died, and 125,000 residents of the affected area have died since the explosion (some reportedly of natural causes). Food resources were ruined, cattle and other livestock were incinerated or genetically damaged. And while Soviet General Secretary Mikhail Gorbachev made no public statements about Chernobyl until May 14 of that year, the U.S. wheat market made the most potent comments about the disaster long before the Soviet leadership felt obliged to recognize its significance (20).

Even before anyone was aware of the size and scope of Chernobyl's meltdown, the wheat market was on the move. Prices vaulted higher as vague rumors of a "nuclear event" spread through the markets on the morning of April 28.

According to the Chernobyl Commission Report, the first warning lights were flashed at the Forsmark Nuclear Power Plant, 60 miles north of Stockholm, Sweden. Eventually Finnish authorities would report that radioactive gases were entering their airspace as they crossed the Russian border (21).

Alert traders in the Chicago grain pits bought wheat by the bushel, correctly assuming that the path being cut by the radioactive cloud could be traced back to the Ukraine, which has long been the breadbasket of Russia. Indeed, the Ukraine is to Russia what the heartland is to America: the principal area where much of the nation's agricultural commodities are produced.

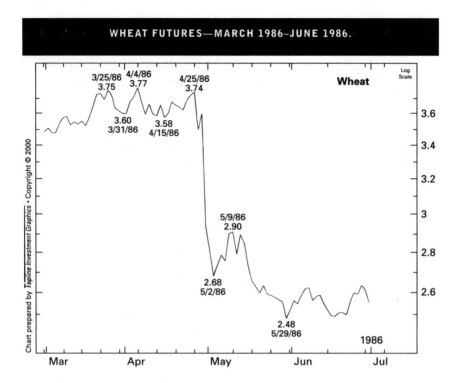

WHEAT FUTURES—MARCH 1986–JUNE 1986.

A nuclear accident, no matter how small, had the potential to destroy crops and livestock for years to come. Such a development would force the Soviet Union to frantically import grain, particularly wheat, to make bread, the favorite foodstuff of the Russian proletariat. This was the thinking on the morning of April 28. Traders reacted far more quickly than the news leaked out.

It would be days before even the partial story of Chernobyl would be told. It would be over a decade before the full extent of the damage would be reported. But in the space of just a few moments after the radioactive fallout was measured in Europe's northernmost countries, the markets of Chicago sent a serious signal about the greatest nuclear accident in the world. And once again, the markets knew of the event long before the rest of the world.

6

Cycle Times

By now, you should be comfortable with the notion that there's nearly nothing you can't learn from watching the markets. Whether it's assessing the direction of the economy, interest rates, industries, or even global geopolitics, markets are important indicators of how the world is turning.

Test out the thesis of this book sometime. Take a few minutes, pick a topic, and see if you can't use the markets to help forecast the future.

Let's say you are interested in fashion. If you'd like to know about the hottest fashions in the season to come, track the stocks of the fashion designers. Does Ralph Lauren (symbol: RL) have the appropriate clothes for the spring season? Is Donna Karan (symbol: DK) ready to make a comeback? What's the Gap (symbol: GPS) got that other specialty retailers haven't got?

The answers to many of these questions probably can be seen in the stock prices of all those firms. Further study of the companies' prospects will tell you even more. The behavior of stock prices, particularly on a relative basis between and among companies and industries, can tell you a lot about how the future will look. Other market indicators can make broader predictions.

The markets can send signals about both economic and noneconomic events. In this chapter, we examine some relatively obscure market indicators that retain some relevance today. While, in a few cases, these indicators may be losing a bit of their predictive power, they bear watching because just when you think an indicator is out of favor, it becomes popular all over again.

But the principle on which even these old school indicators work is still important to understand. They became message makers for a reason.

A Barbarous Relic

The history of gold as an object of both fascination and speculation is a storied one. The lustrous but malleable metal has been prized and cherished since the dawn of time. Scarce and lovely, it has served as an adornment, and as money. From the day Archimedes yelled, "Eureka," in ancient Greece to the gold rush in nineteenth century America to the growing appetite for gold in emerging markets today, the yellow metal has captured the heart, mind, and frequently the pocketbook of nearly every human being who has encountered it.

Gold's importance as a storehouse of value rarely has been disputed, though its significance as a form of money appears in jeopardy in the West today. Still, in some form or another, gold has been a nearly universal store of wealth. Its supply is relatively limited. Its beauty is obvious. It is easier to carry around, in coin form, than loadstones. And it's a better medium of exchange than barter. So it's no wonder that gold has served many useful purposes throughout its history.

Gold's chief role, though, throughout economic history has been as currency. Better able to maintain its value than paper money, gold has been seen as a protector of purchasing power in both good and bad times. Unless purposely debased, gold has provided people all around the world with a store of value that has been unrivalled. Kings and queens filled their treasuries with gold.

Explorers searched the New World for it. Nation-states pegged their currencies to it, while modern central banks store it to support the value of their paper money.

Lately, however, the role of gold in the new economy has changed. Few people believe that gold should still be regarded as anything more than a high-priced commodity. Its monetary value has been eroding as new, higher-yielding, or more complicated financial instruments replace it as a hedge against economic calamity. Throughout the 1990s, central banks from Australia to Austria reduced their gold holdings, pushing down its price and leading some to declare gold completely dead as an investment option.

But regardless of gold's changing role in modern times, it remains useful as an indicator of inflationary pressures in any economy. While some economists doubt that gold can be useful in forecasting important changes in the inflation rate, a careful study of gold prices shows that the so-called barbarous relic still has some functionality. Economist Jason Trennert points out that despite its tarnished reputation as an indicator, the movement in the price of gold has accurately forecast the direction of interest rates one year hence, in 15 of the last 19 years.

Even in ancient times, gold prices and inflation have been tightly correlated, but for reasons slightly different than we find today. In Rome, great inflations occurred when the Roman government debased its own coins by mixing other metals in with gold. Debasement devalued the coins so that it took more Roman coins to buy the same amount of goods as a solid gold piece once did. Put another way, prices rose as a consequence of the devaluation. And that, very simply, is inflation.

Future societies suffered similarly when they devalued the coins of the realm. Economic history is replete with examples of such currency debasement and subsequent inflationary spirals.

In many cases, debasement of the currency and the attendant rise in inflation led to catastrophic bouts of social unrest. We see that today, still. In 1997, a paper currency crisis in Asia led to hyperinflation and severe recessions throughout the Pacific Rim. The troubling times gave way, almost immediately, to massive protests, outbursts of violence, and political upheaval in Thailand, Malaysia and, especially, Indonesia in the late 1990s. As a consequence, the price of gold skyrocketed in those countries as their currencies plunged in value. Asian citizens, fearful of a debilitating loss of purchasing power, bought gold in a panic to protect whatever money they had left.

Despite denials by economists, the link between gold and inflation, and the value of gold as a key indicator, appear to be intact.

The most telling example of that link exists in our own recent past. Recall that only 20 years ago inflation threatened the U.S. economy in the 1970s and early 1980s. By 1980, the inflation rate in the United States had climbed into double digits, peaking at about 13 percent. In other words, the average citizen required a 13 percent pay hike every year just to keep up with the rising cost of living! If inflation continued at that pace, the cost of living would have doubled every six years in the United States. Compare that with how we live today, when inflation has been rising by less than 2 percent a year for the last several years. If inflation rose 2 percent a year steadily, it would take *36* years for the cost of living to double.

In both those economic environments, the price of gold had not just responded accordingly, but actually anticipated the changes in the underlying inflation rate.

The price action of gold told investors that inflation was an intensifying problem throughout the 1970s and had peaked in 1980. Had any investors or consumers been paying attention to gold's price, they would have profited handsomely in both environments.

Remember that gold is among the few commodities that can maintain a constant value in both inflationary and deflationary times. As its price rises and falls, an ounce of gold can buy virtually the same items in any environment. Indeed, many Wall Street investors know that historically an ounce of gold is worth the cost of a good suit. (In late 1999, the price of gold was roughly $290 an ounce. The average price for a man's suit was roughly the same.)

But getting back to gold's predictive powers, a chart of gold shows clearly how gold predicted rising and falling inflation in the last 30 years or so. To see that we must look at a slightly longer-term history of the yellow metal. For much of this country's history, the price of gold was fixed in value. The United States spent much of its history on the gold standard. The gold standard allowed any citizen to redeem paper money, or dollars, for a fixed amount of gold anytime and anywhere. The currency was then deemed "good as gold" because it could never be devalued as long as it was convertible into a fixed amount of gold. Under the best possible circumstances, a dollar would *always* equal a certain amount of gold. And that was true until President Franklin D. Roosevelt partially abandoned the gold standard in the 1930s. Until that time, the U.S. government fixed the price of gold at roughly $21 an ounce. For some complicated reasons that exchange rate was raised in 1934 to $35 an ounce. It remained there until 1971.

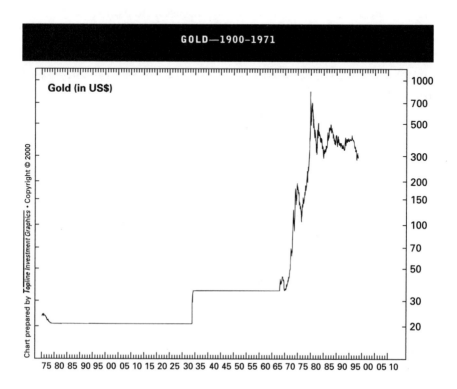

Since the dollar and gold were linked, gold was not very useful as an inflation indicator. Its price never changed, so it sent no helpful price signals to investors, as commodities do in free-market environments.

But in 1971, an embattled President Richard Nixon took the United States off the gold standard. Again, for very complex reasons, the United States had accumulated deficits larger than its supply of gold. That meant foreign interests held dollars that were redeemable for gold on demand. But since they owned more dollars than there was gold, the Nixon administration feared that foreigners could essentially raid Fort Knox, wiping out the supply of U.S. gold.

So to make a long story short, Nixon abandoned the gold standard in 1971, allowing both the dollar and gold to float freely. Henceforth, the financial markets would determine the price of an ounce of gold and the exchange rate of the dollar. Not coincidentally, of course, the value of the dollar promptly plunged since it was no longer backed by gold. The United States then suffered the beginnings of an inflationary spiral that would last nine painful years.

Gold's price took off like a rocket as inflation heated up. By 1980, gold had topped $800 per ounce. Traders, investors, and even consumers scrambled to buy gold at any price as an investment, or sold precious family heirlooms just to cash in on the rising price of gold. As precious metals careened higher in price, many forecasters predicted that gold would hit $1000 an ounce and then move higher still. But the market began to send a completely different message.

Almost as quickly as it rose to staggering heights, gold began a rapid descent. In 1980, the price of gold crashed just as inflation was reaching its peak. Long-term interest rates crested as gold topped out. Those markets responded quickly to the message sent by then Federal Reserve Board chairman, Paul Volcker. The imposingly tall and rather formidable Fed chief dramatically raised interest rates in an effort to cool an overheating U.S. economy and drive inflation out of the system. His efforts proved heroic and the U.S. economy, after a punishing recession, emerged as a solid, more stable, and more dynamic system than ever before. The crash in the price of gold, a long-time inflation hedge, signaled that the days of inflation, stagflation, and recession were over.

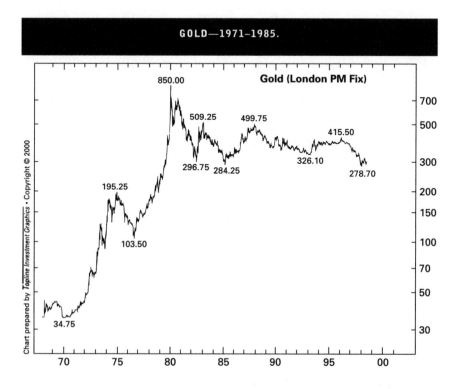

To this very day, despite the doubts of economists, gold has been sending accurate signals about the prospects for inflation. Since 1985, gold prices have been cut in half again, reaching a low of $250 per ounce in the summer of 1999. Inflation rates, meanwhile, have moved steadily lower ever since.

The correlation between gold prices and inflation is still remarkably tight. While many pundits have suggested that gold's link to inflation is dead, it's quite obvious that that is simply not true. Gold may have a reduced role in the world economy. It may no longer be a viable currency. But since gold is a commodity that remains quite sensitive to fluctuations in the value of paper currencies around the world, it's not yet time to ignore the message of this market. Remember, always listen to the markets before you listen to the experts!*

Copper Top

There's an old saying on Wall Street: "The economy is topped with a copper roof." It's a strange saying that doesn't make a lot of sense without a brief explanation. But its meaning is legend on the street.

Just after World War II, the U.S. economy was almost totally driven by the manufacturing sector. As baby boomers returned from war, settled down, and started families, the economy mushroomed into a new age. Manufacturing activity exploded. The boomers moved to the suburbs to buy new homes. They furnished the homes with shiny, new, state-of-the-art appliances. After years of sacrifice during the war, where the auto industry's efforts were diverted toward the military effort, auto sales accelerated like never before. Every new house needed a telephone since the United States was wired for sound.

In 1946, manufacturing activity accounted for nearly half of America's gross national product. One key commodity that was (and still is) used in the building of durable goods was copper. Copper was used for electrical wiring in new homes. Copper was a key commodity in auto assembly, in appliance production, and in the upgrading of the country's growing telephone network.

Like oil, copper was an increasingly ubiquitous commodity. Hence, the price of copper, like any other commodity, was quite sensitive to demand. And in the postwar years, demand for all sorts of goods and services exploded. So, then, did the price of copper.

---

*NOTE: Art Cashin, PaineWebber's director of floor operations at the New York Stock Exchange, shares this story about gold. As a young man, Art was reminded about gold's important characteristics by one of his many mentors, an elderly Eastern European man who had lived through the terrible times in the middle of the twentieth century. Gold was so valuable it could save someone's life even during the most dangerous moments. The old man admonished Art, "Always keep enough gold to bribe the border guards!" To this day, some people keep a little gold on hand, just in case.

As the economy grew rapidly in the early years of the baby boom era, copper prices rallied smartly. And it was a drop in the price of copper that oftentimes signaled an imminent recession. When copper prices peaked, that peak usually coincided with a peak in economic activity.

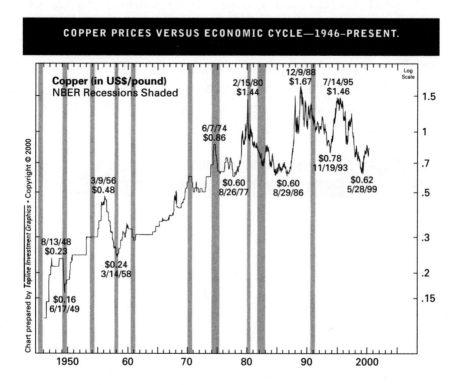

COPPER PRICES VERSUS ECONOMIC CYCLE—1946–PRESENT.

The price of copper may not have as strong a predictive power as it once did, but the relationship between copper prices and economic cycles remained quite strong until just a few years ago. As the chart illustrates, copper prices tended to peak just before a recession began and recovered just before the subsequent recovery got started. The sneak peak, if you will, in copper prices led to the notion that the economy was "topped with a copper roof."

The link between a peak in copper prices and a peak in the economic cycle has become somewhat more tenuous in the United States. Manufacturing accounts for less than 18 percent of gross domestic product. The service sector, which doesn't use a lot of copper, represents the bulk of modern economic activity, at least domestically. But the link between copper and the manufacturing sector remains as strong as ever.

Consider the behavior of copper prices in the months before the Asian economic crisis. Copper prices were quite strong, as booming Asian and Latin American economies boosted demand for all sorts of manufactured goods. Many of the newly industrialized Asian countries had vibrant technology sectors that were rapidly increasing their output of computers and other high technology goods. Copper is used abundantly in the manufacture of computers and related products. As a consequence, copper prices were surging in the spring of 1997.

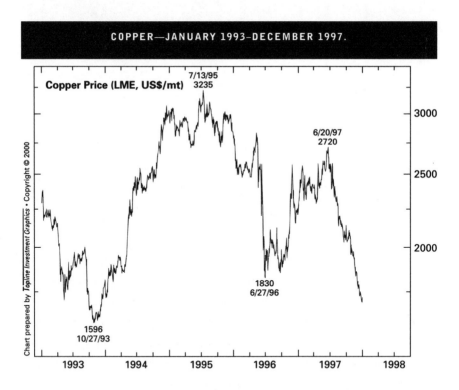

COPPER—JANUARY 1993–DECEMBER 1997.

Copper prices rose until the summer when the first signs of the crisis began to emerge. The devaluation of the Thai baht, as we discussed before, sent the first signal that Asia's high flying economies were in danger of collapsing. A nearly simultaneous decline in the price of copper was another early warning signal that the global economy was topped with a copper roof.

So swift and so severe was the Asian crisis that copper prices collapsed completely in 1998. A pound of copper, which sold for as much as $1.40 in mid-1997, crashed in price to $ .68 per pound in a matter of months. The plunge in copper prices was accompanied by a disastrous decline in the prices of many other commodities. Industrial metals like zinc, nickel, and aluminum fell in tandem with copper. As economic activity throughout the Pacific Rim came to a standstill, demand for industrial commodities dried up completely. Copper led them into their death spiral.

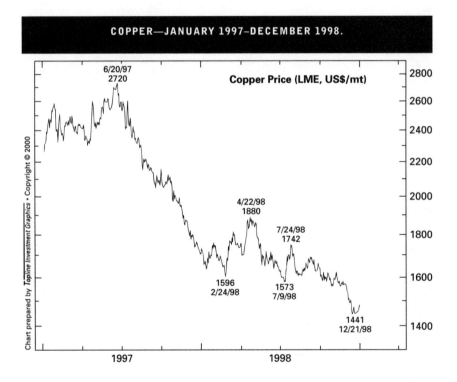

Oil prices also traced out a similar pattern. Indeed, oil's collapse may have been even more telling than the decline in copper prices.

The *Journal of Commerce*'s Spot Commodity Index illustrates the severe decline in the prices of industrial commodities that followed in copper's wake.

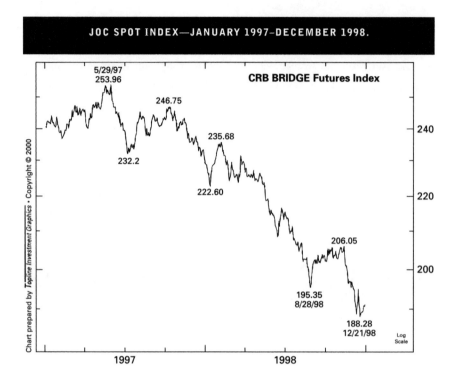

JOC SPOT INDEX—JANUARY 1997–DECEMBER 1998.

Many Asian countries, like Japan, are huge importers of oil. Others, like Indonesia, are major oil exporters. The calamitous drop in oil prices reflected an immediate drop in oil demand in Asia while putting further economic pressure on the already devastated economy of Indonesia.

The 50 percent declines in key industrial commodity prices told the world that a significant economic event was taking place around the world. Declines that severe don't happen without proper justification. While the collapse of commodity prices reflected the severity of the global economic crisis in late 1997 and in 1998, the commodity bust was a boon to the American consumer.

Certainly the deflationary pulse that swept the global economy was hurtful to the commodity-producing nations of the developing world. But to a major commodity consumer like the United States, the drop in the prices of manufactured goods gave new life to the

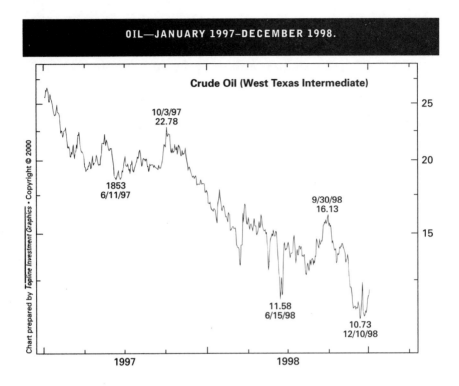

OIL—JANUARY 1997–DECEMBER 1998.

Crude Oil (West Texas Intermediate)

10/3/97
22.78

1853
6/11/97

9/30/98
16.13

11.58
6/15/98

10.73
12/10/98

1997   1998

Chart prepared by *Topline Investment Graphics* · Copyright © 2000

U.S. economy. Gasoline prices collapsed. The cost of high-quality imported goods declined sharply. Interest rates in the United States plunged as inflation virtually disappeared.

All of those developments were foretold by a curious collapse in copper prices in the summer of 1997. However, in an increasingly interconnected, complex, service-oriented, and global economy, the price of a single commodity can no longer have the same predictive powers that it once had. But a basket of commodity prices, like the Journal of Commerce Index or the C-R-B Index, can still give investors and consumers an important "heads up" about the arc of an economic cycle. Some economists still call the red metal *Dr. Copper*, thanks to its time-tested diagnostic capabilities.

For anyone who remembered Wall Street's simple old saying, "The economy is topped with a copper roof," the summer of 1997 was golden.

The Presidential Cycle

The financial markets can be quite useful in anticipating changes in the economy, but the stock market can even predict important political events, as well. There is sufficient evidence that the stock market knows who the next U.S. president will be nearly a full year before the November elections. It is an indicator that, as our charts will show, is rarely wrong.

It is important to remember that the stock market is a so-called discounting mechanism. The smart money crowd makes big and usually informed bets on the likely outcome of many different events. Those bets show up in the prices of stocks, bonds, and commodities and are generally priced in long before the event actually occurs.

Take, for example, the trials and tribulations of President William Jefferson Clinton. While Main Street suffered through the agonizing political process that involved the Ken Starr investigation of Whitewater and Monica Lewinsky, and the president's ultimate impeachment in the House of Representatives, Wall Street reacted only sporadically to the dizzying spectacle that consumed Washington in 1998.

To be sure, as various revelations about the president's peccadilloes leaked out, the stock market dipped as traders cast and recast their votes on the possibility the president would be removed from office. But overall the stock market remained remarkably calm throughout the president's darkest days. In fact, 1998 was one of the best years of the 1990s for Wall Street. Many would argue that Wall Street insiders knew how this high political drama would play out. Many of the most informed investors and traders with whom I spoke during those days had gathered remarkable bits of intelligence long before the press got a hold of them. Graphic details about the president's encounters with Monica Lewinsky were obtained by many well-heeled investors, long before they were discussed on the nightly news, printed in newspapers or, finally, made public in the Starr Report.

You may wonder how or why Wall Street types were so interested in getting the latest dish on President Clinton. It's very simple; knowledge isn't just power, it's money. If an investor learns of a development that might alter the course of expected events, he or she can make a profitable trade based on that knowledge. And so the market suffered through many twists and turns as the smart money crowd picked up new tidbits and traded them throughout the other "trial of the century."

Aside from the wiggles and squiggles in the market, day to day, the truly informed money made the right bet that the president's impeachment would not lead to removal from office. In the tense days leading up to the impeachment vote and the subsequent Senate trial, the stock market was unusually calm.

The big decline in the stock market, while worsened by the uncertainty that shrouded the White House at the time, was the result of the Russian debt default and the collapse of Long-Term Capital Management, the hedge fund that lost billions in the global financial markets.

Wall Street sailed through the impeachment process while Washington was mired in it. Wall Street has looked through other major events and has reacted violently to still others. The Watergate scandal and President Nixon's resignation sent the stock market into a tailspin, although stocks began to recover from a punishing bear market as the "long national nightmare" came to a close.

Wall Street was suffering through economic difficulties at the time as well. Inflation was on the rise after the Arab oil embargo, so both Wall Street and Main Street were in no mood to tolerate political problems, as well. (Fortunately for Bill Clinton, his scandal and impeachment came during one of the strongest economies of modern times. Many argue that had there been economic troubles at home at the time, the stock market and the voters would have punished the president more severely.)

While Wall Street has sent clear messages to Washington about politics, policy, and scandal, its best message may be sent to the public about 11 months before a presidential election. Jim Stack,

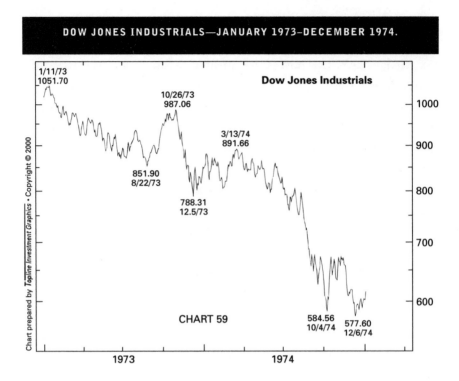

DOW JONES INDUSTRIALS—JANUARY 1973–DECEMBER 1974.

1/11/73
1051.70

Dow Jones Industrials

10/26/73
987.06

3/13/74
891.66

851.90
8/22/73

788.31
12.5/73

CHART 59

584.56
10/4/74

577.60
12/6/74

1000

900

800

700

600

1973   1974

Chart prepared by *Topline Investment Graphics* • Copyright © 2000

the editor and publisher of the *InvesTech* stock market newsletter, has done exhaustive research on the relationship between Wall Street and the White House. He has written, rather convincingly, that the road to the White House intersects Wall Street. In almost every presidential election in this century, the party in power maintained power or was shown the door depending on how the stock market behaved 11 months before the election. If the Dow Jones Industrial Average falls 10 percent or more early in the election year, it is highly probable a new president will be elected in November. Conversely, if the Dow is rallying to new highs in that period, the party, if not the person, in power wins the election.

Indeed, there are very few instances in which a rising market failed to help an incumbent candidate and a falling market failed to do him in. It can be argued that the truly devastating declines in the stock market were sending signals to Washington policymakers that something was terribly wrong with the economy. In the cases of

Herbert Hoover, Richard Nixon, and Jimmy Carter, trouble on Wall Street predicted their departures from Pennsylvania Avenue.

InvesTech's Jim Stack has also studied the history of stock market cycles within a presidential term. While this aspect of the market's behavior does not conform, necessarily, to the premise of this book, it is an interesting and related phenomenon. It appears that the stock market has a behavior pattern that is remarkably repetitious in any president's term. Bear markets tend to occur in the first year or two of the new president, while bull markets tend to occur in the middle and end of a term.

The reason for this relatively fixed pattern of behavior is quite simple. Most presidents are willing to take the nasty medicine of reform, both economic and political, in the first two years of their terms. In the second half of the term the president is attempting to either get reelected or get his vice president elected to extend the party's grip on power. As a consequence, a lot of "pump-priming" to rev up the economy is done closer to election time.

In recent years, that cycle has been violated somewhat. In normal times, the Federal Reserve frequently is cutting interest rates later in a president's term in an effort to jump-start the economy, Jim found. As Ronald Reagan learned in 1983 and 1984, the improvement in the economy was strong enough to propel him back into office by a substantial margin of victory.

Conversely, President George Bush (some people say) is still fuming that Fed chief Alan Greenspan raised rates in late 1989 and 1990. The higher rates, along with rising oil prices from the Gulf War, helped to cause a recession that did not seem to end until Bill Clinton was elected in 1992. (In reality, the recession ended in 1991, but very few Americans felt any improvement in their situations until much later.)

Generally, however, the presidential cycle studied by Jim Stack and market historian Yale Hirsch remains intact to this day.

If you're trying to bet on who will be president in the next election, Wall Street generally knows the answer. If the market is hitting new all-time highs 10 or 11 months before election day, the incumbent will win. If the market is 10 percent or more below its high and falling 11 months before the polls open, look for the challenger to take the White House.

NOTE: In March 2000, the market was sending a mixed message about the upcoming presidential election. While the Dow Jones Industrial Average was off more than 15 percent from its January 14th high of 11,722, the NASDAQ Composite was up almost 25 percent, quite close to its record above 5000. If the Dow holds sway, and presages a downturn in the economy, Al Gore could conceivably lose the White House. If the new economy NASDAQ is right, then the self-proclaimed inventor of the Internet may become the 42nd president of the United States.

For the truly avid political junkie, the Iowa Political Stock Market makes markets from presidential contenders. In that market, you can keep a running tally on who's leading whom going into the elections!

The Tower of Babel

*"Then they said, 'Come, let us build ourselves a city and a tower whose top may reach to heaven; and let us make a name for ourselves, lest we be scattered abroad upon the face of the whole earth.'
And the Lord came down to see the city and the tower which men were building.
And the Lord said, 'Behold they are one people and they all have one language; and they have reasoned to do this thing; and now nothing will prevent them from doing that which they have imagined to do.' "*

Genesis 4:7

E ver since the days of Genesis, humankind has aspired to reach for the heavens through nonspiritual venues, even if those aspirations were not kindly looked upon by God. The sin of hubris among the Babel builders was punished swiftly by the Lord, who scattered the people and scrambled their one language into many.

Curiously enough, today it seems that there is still a hefty price to pay for erecting buildings that climb to the heavens, though the penalty may be only economic rather than spiritual. There is a rather odd indicator that has a revelation-like power to predict the onset of a stock market top. And it's associated with humanity's eternal climb toward the heavens.

The folks at the Elliott Wave Theorist, a financial market research service founded by 1980s stock market guru Robert Prechter, have long tracked the relationship between rising buildings and rising stock prices. As was the case in the Genesis story, pride, here too, goeth before the fall.

The Elliott Wave researchers credit Edward R. Dewey with discovering the "skyscraper indicator," which associates the construction of the world's tallest buildings with major stock market tops. Those who constantly search for market messages often look to areas that aren't markets per se, but instead are subsectors within a market, as skyscrapers would be a subsector of the construction market. The skyscraper indicator has an uncanny knack for predicting the end of major bull market moves.

Consider New York in the early 1900s. Manhattan was just beginning its rise to prominence as the world's financial capital. London was, of course, still the financial world's preeminent city, but New York was well on its way to conquering the world of finance.

According to the Elliott Wave Theorist, the Woolworth building was begun in 1906, just a year before the panic of 1907. Very few people today understand the seriousness of that panic, which threatened Wall Street's very existence. As crowds mobbed the lower portion of Manhattan, filling Wall and Broad Streets, the elder J.P. Morgan rescued the market with a valiant purchase of equities. The panic arrived as New York's tallest building was being put in place.

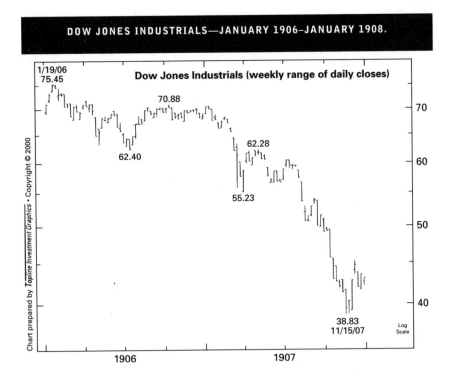

DOW JONES INDUSTRIALS—JANUARY 1906–JANUARY 1908.

In the 1920s, again, New York broke ground on buildings that would vie for the title of "tallest in the world." The Chrysler

Building, whose art deco facade still graces the New York City sky-
line, and the Empire State Building, which requires no description,
were erected in 1929. The competition was so fierce to gain the
"tallest" title that the Empire State builders added a spire to the top
of the structure to push it past its uptown rival.

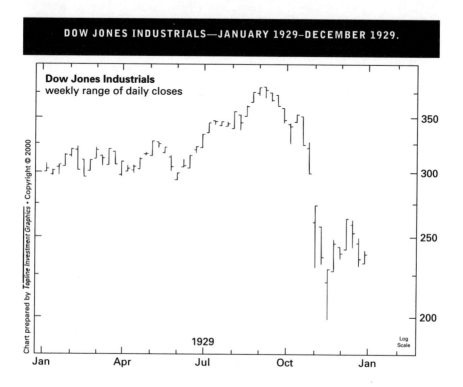

DOW JONES INDUSTRIALS—JANUARY 1929–DECEMBER 1929.

The market historians at Elliott Wave quote a graceful passage
from the *New Republic* in July 1931, reflecting on the significance
of humanity's attempt to climb a physical stairway to heaven: "The
material embodiment of the late bull market remains in our metro-
politan structures of towering heights. They soar boldly above a surrounding mesa of roofs, very much as the spirelike graph of 1929
equity prices. The same causes explain both pinnacles."

In 1966, the foundation for the World Trade Center was being
poured as the Dow approached 1000 for the first time ever. The
twin towers represented the twin assaults the Dow would make on
1000 in 1966 and 1968, only to fail to penetrate that important

millennial milestone. It would be several years before the Dow would make an assault on 1000 again and it would not break through that level in a meaningful way until 1984.

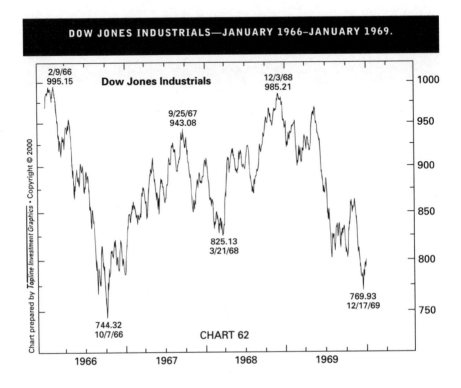

DOW JONES INDUSTRIALS—JANUARY 1966–JANUARY 1969.

2/9/66
995.15   **Dow Jones Industrials**   12/3/68
                                        985.21   1000

                        9/25/67
                        943.08   950

                                                                        900

                                                                        850

                                825.13
                                3/21/68   800

                                                        769.93
                                                        12/17/69   750

744.32
10/7/66   CHART 62

1966   1967   1968   1969

Chart prepared by *Topline Investment Graphics* • Copyright © 2000

The Sears Tower jutted out onto Chicago's lakefront in January 1973, just as the stock market roared to a peak. The Dow would suffer cataclysmic setbacks in 1973 and 1974 and drop still lower until its ultimate bottom at 777 in the summer of 1982.

Eerily, Malaysian officials began constructing the Petronas Towers in 1996. Those skyscrapers command the world's tallest title today but were still being built as the Asian economic crisis cratered the economies of Thailand, Indonesia, Korea, Hong Kong and, of course, Malaysia. In July 1997, the crisis began to unfold. By autumn of that year, Malaysia's currency and stock markets collapsed. Its economy crumbled under the yoke of heavy foreign debt and has not yet fully recovered.

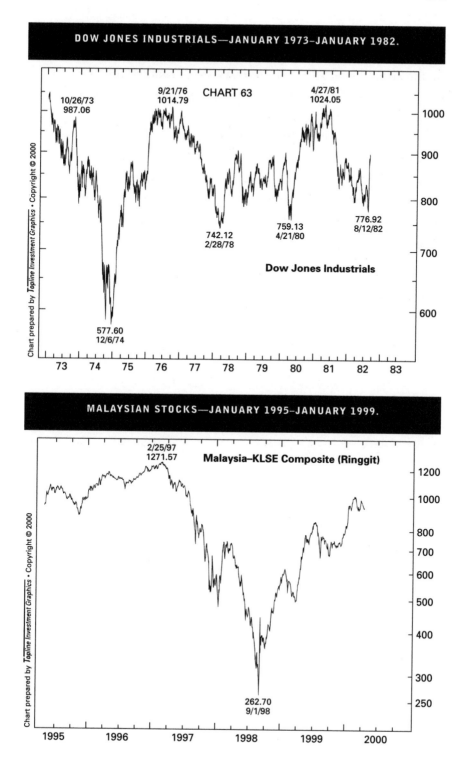

DOW JONES INDUSTRIALS—JANUARY 1973–JANUARY 1982.

10/26/73
987.06

9/21/76
1014.79

CHART 63

4/27/81
1024.05

776.92
8/12/82

742.12
2/28/78

759.13
4/21/80

Dow Jones Industrials

577.60
12/6/74

Chart prepared by *Topline Investment Graphics* • Copyright © 2000

73 74 75 76 77 78 79 80 81 82 83

MALAYSIAN STOCKS—JANUARY 1995–JANUARY 1999.

2/25/97
1271.57

Malaysia–KLSE Composite (Ringgit)

262.70
9/1/98

Chart prepared by *Topline Investment Graphics* • Copyright © 2000

1995   1996   1997   1998   1999   2000

Coincidentally, Indonesia's government was embarking on a project to build the world's *longest* building, a mile long structure, in the summer of 1997. Indonesia's stock market collapsed by 90 percent in the Asian crisis. Plans to complete the building were immediately suspended.

Even more ominously today, several cities of the world are contemplating erecting new structures of commanding heights. In Shanghai and Chicago, the race is on again. The message may be clear that Chinese and American markets are living on borrowed time, destined to be toppled, even as their buildings stretch ever closer to heaven.

7

Modern Times

We have spent much of this book exploring how markets have sent messages throughout time. It's clear, with the benefit of 20/20 hindsight, that markets do flash warning signals and often send accurate signals about impending events. An even more detailed account of market history, of the behavior of individual stocks, bonds, or commodities, would reveal innumerable examples of this phenomenon.

The emergence of railroad stocks in the 1850s and their proliferation and outstanding performances into the early 1900s sent very strong messages about how the rail system would transform the way America lived, traveled and, most important, conducted business. The radio stocks sent their own signals about the emergence of a transformational communications medium that radically altered the fabric of American society. So, too, the behavior of auto stocks at the turn of the last century, phone stocks circa 1900, computer stocks in the early 1980s, or Internet stocks at the end of the 1990s.

A more challenging exercise today is to heed the message of the modern markets. What is Wall Street telling us? Has the nature of economic life changed so dramatically at the end of the twentieth century that investors are selling their old economy stocks to finance the purchase of new economy darlings? Federal Reserve

Chairman Alan Greenspan noted publicly that once in a lifetime epochal changes to the economy occur, in which massive technological innovation heralds the dawn of a new day. In congressional testimony and in other public pronouncements, Mr. Greenspan held out the possibility that we may be witnessing just such a rare phenomenon today.

In the next section, we examine how the markets may be trying to communicate that notion to us now. Whether the new paradigm is hope, hype, or simply hogwash remains to be seen. But given the vast implications for economic growth, job creation, and a major advancement in living standards and quality of life, this is one message that will be worth listening to in the months and years ahead.

NASDAQ Attack

There are times in history when the stock market sends very clear messages. There are other times, however, when the market's message may be quite ambiguous and becomes obvious only in retrospect. We've already seen pretty potent examples of the former, but only an example or two of the latter.

In 1999, the NASDAQ stock market sent a host of signals to investors, but which signal was the one correctly forecasting the future remains to be seen. There are two options. Either the NASDAQ's gains accurately predicted the rise of the new economy, in which high-tech, Internet, fiber optic, and biotechnology companies were poised to replace the old economy, built on steel, bricks and mortar, and professional services. Or, the run-up in NASDAQ stocks was among the great speculative episodes in stock market history that will be remembered like the market manias of days gone by.

In calendar 1999 the NASDAQ Composite, the index that captures the action in all 4500 NASDAQ stocks, skyrocketed by better than 85 percent. That was the "Comp's" best year ever. In fact, it was the best performance of a major U.S. stock market average since the Dow Industrials gained 81 percent in 1915! The gain eclipsed the 56 percent rally that the NASDAQ enjoyed in 1991, as the U.S. economy emerged from the Gulf War–induced recession. By March of 2000, the NASDAQ added another 25 percent. It was a performance rarely witnessed in the annals of financial market history.

Many times stock market averages explode at the end of recession, just as the NASDAQ Composite did in 1991. But what is the message of the NASDAQ stock market in 1999 and 2000, fully eight years into an economic recovery and, arguably, much closer to the recovery's end than its beginning?

There are many observers of the modern economic scene who suggest that the phenomenal performance of the stock market in the mid- to late-1990s is the result of a new economic paradigm. The *new paradigmers,* as they are called, theorize that stock market returns have been higher in the 1990s than in almost any other decade, on average, because the economy is growing quite briskly without generating a menacing increase in inflationary pressures. What is the reason for that? Technological innovation. The rapid improvement in technology has driven up productivity so quickly that inflation has remained under control even as the economy grew at a seemingly unsustainable pace.

And what does that have to do with the NASDAQ? The NASDAQ Composite Index is chock full of technology company stocks. In fact, the world's most valuable company, Microsoft, trades on the NASDAQ. So do other high flying tech stocks, like Intel, Cisco Systems, Dell Computer, Sun Microsystems, MCI Worldcom, and Qualcomm. Those companies are at the leading edge of the technological revolution, providing everything from software to microchips and the routers, switchers, and telephone lines that make the Internet work.

The Internet explosion in 1999 fueled massive gains in the revenue, profits, and stock prices of many of the big high-tech companies, despite the mounting losses of the freshly minted Internet companies themselves. The big companies that provide the backbone for Internet service and for its handmaiden, wireless communications, also enjoyed spectacular growth and phenomenal increases in stock market value.

The gains in the NASDAQ's big five—Microsoft, Cisco, Intel, Dell, and MCI Worldcom—were largely responsible for the NASDAQ's record year. By the end of 1999, the market value of all NASDAQ stocks was $5.2 trillion. The big five accounted for roughly 30 percent of that value. The other 4495 stocks made up the rest.

There is an important reason for the explosive performance of those five stocks. They were (and still are) the direct beneficiaries of the "wired world." (Microsoft cofounder Paul Allen, also the third richest man in America, envisions a world where everyone has full access to advanced communications through his wired world. Allen has invested accordingly in wireless communications, cable TV, and other high-technology ventures.) The wired world, as it is being built, is a boon to companies that build the infrastructure of the future, just as phone companies, construction companies, and electrical companies benefited from the building of America's more traditional infrastructure.

Many observers suggested that the build-out of the wired world would continue for years to come, offering that as justification for the monumental increase in the stock prices of many NASDAQ companies. If they are correct in their assumptions, the bull market in high-tech stocks could continue well into the next century. If they are wrong, however, history suggests that the new paradigm and wired world theses of 1999 could merely have been rationalizations for a stock market euphoria that has seen no modern parallel.

Consider some of the following statistics:

For an unprecedented five years, from 1995 to 2000, the major stock market averages rose better than 20 percent in each of those five years. That had never happened in any previous five-year period.

In 1999, the NASDAQ Composite jumped an astonishing 85 percent, its biggest gain ever. Only five stocks accounted for better than half of the gain. From the stock market's low point in October 1998, the NASDAQ Composite jumped 130 percent, more than doubling in just 14 months. (Even more surprising was the fact that the NASDAQ doubled and the Dow gained better than 60 percent as long-term interest rates rose from 4.7 percent to 6.3 percent.)

The average initial public offering (IPO) gained 60 percent on its first day of trading in 1999 compared to only 10 percent in the years from 1988 to 1998.

Volatility in the stock market increased markedly in 1999 as the NASDAQ moved more than 2 percent, up or down, on more days than in any other year.

The NASDAQ scored 60 record closing highs in 1999, itself a record.

By the end of 1999, the market value of all NASDAQ stocks was $5.2 trillion. The NASDAQ alone was worth more than all the stocks traded on the Tokyo Stock Exchange at its peak at the end of 1989. (Japan's stock market bubble is considered the greatest market bubble of all time.)

The average price/earnings (P/E) ratio of all NASDAQ stocks at year-end 1999 was about 200. In other words, the stocks of the NASDAQ Composite sold at 200 times their earnings—a valuation benchmark higher than in any previous period in world stock market history. That's higher than the P/E ratio of 100 accorded to Japan's market at its peak in 1989. Of the NASDAQ stocks that actually produce earnings, the average P/E ratio was 40 at year-end 1999, suggesting that valuations were high, even among profitable companies.

In addition to the sky-high valuations and stunningly narrow concentration of gains in just a handful of NASDAQ stocks, volatility in individual issues neared record levels. On some days, NASDAQ investors encountered incredibly wild swings in their stocks. It was not unusual to see individual issues move 40, 50, or even 100 points in a single day. The NASDAQ itself routinely moved in 200-point ranges daily. Two and three percent moves for the index became commonplace.

To be fair, while the gains in the NASDAQ, its overall valuation, and its average price/earnings ratio surpassed those of the most speculative bubble of all time in Tokyo over a decade ago, there are some mitigating factors that might suggest the game is not over quite yet.

At its all-time high, the value of all Japanese stocks was equal to more than half the market capitalization of the entire planet at that time. According to Jeff Applegate, the chief market strategist at Lehman Brothers, Japan's market cap accounted for 51 percent of the world's total market value in 1989, but Japan's corporations captured only less than half of all profits produced.

Conversely, while the combined market value of the NASDAQ and the much bigger New York Stock Exchange accounted for more than half the market capitalization of world stock markets in 1999, U.S. companies also earned more than half of all profits among publicly traded global firms. As a consequence, Applegate argued that the high valuations placed on U.S. stocks were, at least partially, justified because U.S. companies held a commensurate share of global profits.

Still, despite justifications and rationalizations, the student of market history was required to ponder the message of the NASDAQ in late 1999. Were the gains on Wall Street supported by real world achievements on Main Street? Or were investors betting the ranch on an "if come" basis, paying high prices for future profits that may never materialize?

Stock market bubbles are hard to spot and even harder to escape since "the lure of easy money has a very strong appeal," to borrow a phrase from Glenn Frey's song, "The Smuggler's Blues." Even the highly regarded chairman of the Federal Reserve, Alan Greenspan, has admitted that it's impossible to identify a stock market bubble while its happening. Bubbles, he has stated publicly, make themselves known only in retrospect.

However, it does help an investor to know if a market is sending bubble messages while the bubble is expanding. In the late 1980s, it became increasingly obvious that the Tokyo Stock Exchange was home to one of the biggest speculative episodes of all time. Stock and real estate prices climbed parabolically and in tandem. Needless to say, the gains in many NASDAQ-traded Internet start-ups have produced hundreds, if not thousands, of paper millionaires who are bidding up property prices to astronomical levels from Silicon Valley to Silicon Alley. In 1999 alone, New York City's controller, Allan Hevesi, estimated that Wall Street would pay out a staggering $13 billion in bonuses—$13 billion! It's not surprising that New York City was booming late in the decade as rents and real estate values set new records regularly. The frenetic trading action generated by newly minted day traders helped drive the market, particularly the NASDAQ, to innumerable new highs in 1999.

Whether the action in the NASDAQ was sending a warning sign of an overinflated stock market was unclear at the time. Indeed, the explosive growth of new technologies and technology-driven services suggested that the world was on the cusp of a new wave of prosperity driven by rapid technological change and a rapid deployment of same. The wired and wireless worlds promised to again shrink the globe and make communications and commerce far more efficient and far more profitable for businesses and consumers alike.

Or maybe, just maybe, the impact of the change was dramatically oversold to Main Street by the Wall Street community. In other words, the new revolution may turn out to be far more sizzle than steak. In any case, the market was sending a message at the end of 1999 that forced investors to make a difficult and potentially costly choice: either to believe the first message that the revolution had only just begun and buy everything associated with it at any price, or to take one's profits from Microsoft, Cisco, Dell, and Qualcomm and run. And run fast before everyone else figures out that the *promise* of prosperity was worth a great deal more than the real thing.

One has to consider those possibilities even before the message of the market becomes clear. It is by asking questions that the true student of the market can hear what Wall Street is saying, instead of simply being swept away in a euphoric tide.

At the end of 1999, questions had to be asked about the entire market. In the final weeks of December, the stock market began sending unambiguous messages that historically have been associated with market tops. Several traditional warning signs were being flashed, though Wall Street pundits pooh-poohed the caution signs that became increasingly obvious. The point of this discussion will be to illustrate that if the market suffers badly in the year 2000, the market will have sent a potent wake-up call to investors long before the bear began rumbling down Wall Street.

Signs of speculative excesses were abundant at the end of 1999. In addition to the unprecedented 85 percent gain in the NASDAQ Composite discussed previously, the final days of the year were particularly exciting. Two weeks before the holidays, NASDAQ volume exploded to nearly 2 billion shares per day. Volume regularly exceeded 2 billion shares daily in early 2000. While some would argue that record highs accompanied by record volume were a bullish, not bearish, sign, many market analysts made the same argument in the summer of 1987, just before the stock market crashed.

The performance of new public companies, IPOs, set records as well. VA Linux, a maker of the Linux operating system, a computer software system that rivals Microsoft's Windows NT, went public at $30 a share. On its first day, it traded as high as $320 per share before ending the day at $245, a 700 percent gain! The first-day performance was the best ever for a new public offering, topping the performance of TheGlobe.com, which gained 606 percent on its first day earlier that year.

The total number of new stock offerings in 1999 set records as well, as did the amount of money raised by new public firms. In the past, such behavior was a sign of rampant and excessive speculation. Speculation has long been associated with the later, rather than earlier, stages of a bull market.

The warning signs, by the way, were not just flashing in the flashy world of high-technology stocks, the NASDAQ, or the Internet. As the Dow Jones Industrial Average closed in on new highs late in the year, the broad list of stocks traded at the New York Stock Exchange did not fare nearly as well. The NYSE advance/decline line, which

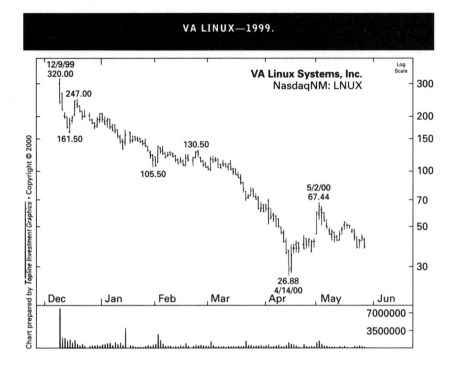

VA LINUX—1999.

VA Linux Systems, Inc.
NasdaqNM: LNUX

Log Scale

12/9/99
320.00

247.00

161.50

130.50

105.50

5/2/00
67.44

26.88
4/14/00

compares the number of stocks going up to the number of stocks going down, had deteriorated significantly.

In simple language, a handful of stocks was driving up the Dow and the NASDAQ while the broad list of stocks was going down. Historically, that has also been a precursor to trouble in the stock market.

Other key market averages also declined as the Dow went up. The Dow Jones Transportation Index plunged nearly 30 percent from its high while the Dow Industrials rallied. The interest rate–sensitive utility and bank indexes also declined sharply late in the year, sending a message that interest rates could climb dangerously higher in the year 2000. (By early 2000, that proved to be a false message. The Dow and the NASDAQ suffered garden-variety corrections early in the year, but there was no market collapse. Interest rates actually fell early in the year, muddling the markets' message to date.) This form of market analysis, known as *technical analysis* on Wall Street, is widely used but is also widely criticized for forecasting more important turns in the market than actually take place.

The weakness of key market averages and other technical indicators sometimes corrects itself. At the end of 1999, it was altogether possible that some of these key technical indicators that were sending seemingly unambiguous negative messages at year-end could turn positive over time.

But, as is their habit in prosperous times, investors become complacent. In an interview with former Treasury Secretary Robert Rubin on CNBC, December 8, 1999, the well-respected Washington and Wall Street veteran warned viewers about that complacency. Rubin said that in ebullient times, investors tend to "underweight risk," meaning they forget that markets go two ways, up *and* down. He added that when speculation becomes excessive, history has taught us that speculative episodes often end unhappily.

If the stock market's action at the end of 1999 was the beginning of the end of this century's greatest bull market, the message was certainly clear. But, once again, the key question remained— was anyone listening?*

Serious students of the market always want to know what "the crowd" is up to. Unlike the smart money, the crowd, or the nonprofessional investor, has long been viewed as "dumb money."

For decades, professionals have thought, rather condescendingly, that the average investor operates at a distinct disadvantage to the better-trained and better-informed professionals. And for much of the financial markets' history, that has been true. It is a long-held belief that by the time the public (the crowd) finds out about and acts on an investment idea, it's time for the professionals to get out.

---

*NOTE: There are times when the real world sends a message about the state of the stock market that can be as important as the messages being sent by the market itself. Astute investors have always studied and assessed mass psychology as a critical determinant in financial market behavior.

The logic of this idea is very simple. Truly informed investors usually can take advantage of their advanced knowledge and act on investment ideas before that same information trickles down to nonprofessional investors. As a new investment idea begins to pan out, the investment begins to rally in price, attracting the attention of more and more professionals, until it is the rally itself (rather than the concept) that draws the public into the game. At that point, professionals unload their shares on the unwitting public, knowing that the lion's share of the gains have already been had. The pros get out just before the concept ceases to work, just as the public is getting in.

The 1990s have made a mockery of the distinction between the smart money and the crowd. In fact, nonprofessional investors have outperformed their better-educated superiors for much of the 1990s.

Yet, investors still study crowd psychology to determine if too many investors are on a particular bandwagon. When everyone is bullish on a particular investment, there is no one left to do the buying that will take that investment still higher. And if everyone is bearish, no one is left to sell. That's why professionals still analyze sentiment indicators and why they often look to the real world for messages about the market.

In the olden days (defined here as any year before 1999), the smart money would often abandon the stock market when a popular magazine like *Time* or *Newsweek* put a bull on the cover of its latest issue. Many veterans believed that by the time a general interest publication decided that stocks would go up forever, the party was about to end. There are investors who have often sold out their entire portfolios based on that indicator alone.

While that is a simplistic view of crowd psychology, it will be interesting to see if America's intense preoccupation with money sent a similar warning signal at the end of 1999.

In the winter of 1999, Americans fell madly in love with two new quiz shows, *Who Wants to Be a Millionaire* and *Greed.* In both programs, contestants had to answer a series of relatively easy questions en route to winning $1 or $2 million. The shows were instant hits on the ABC and Fox television networks, respectively. So intense was the interest in becoming an instant millionaire that for the first time in several years, ABC won the November and February ratings races, all because of Regis Philbin and his million-dollar quiz show.

On February 18, 2000, one day after the NASDAQ closed above 4500 for the first time, the stock market movie *Boiler Room,* with Ben Affleck and Giovanni Rabisi, opened in theatres across the nation. Simultaneously, at least one other market movie was poised for release while two television shows set in stock market trading rooms were in development.

There are times when the real world tells us a lot about market psychology. After a record bull run on Wall Street, after thousands of freshly minted Internet millionaires were created, after a record number of *billionaires* made the pages of the *Forbes* 400, record numbers of people tuned in to see who could win a quick million bucks. The message *about* the market at the end of 1999 may have been just as important as the message *of* the market at the turn of this moneyed century.

One final anecdote on this score . . .

On December 14, 1999, I interviewed stock market specialist and floor broker Peter Henderson. Peter is the managing director of Labranche & Co., a firm that makes markets in several financial stocks listed on the New York Stock Exchange.

In a tale cautiously reminiscent of the old story about Joseph P. Kennedy Sr. and the fabled shoe shine boy, Henderson told me about a man who was homeless and paraplegic and begged for money outside the New York Stock Exchange every day in 1999. Peter had stopped to give the man a dollar every day, as many New Yorkers did. (While the homeless population has declined in the 1990s, there are still plenty of disadvantaged people forced to beg on the streets of Manhattan.) On the morning of December 14, the man stopped Peter as he handed him a dollar, and asked Peter if he was a stock broker. Peter said, "Yes. I am." The homeless man then asked Peter about an Internet stock that he'd heard about and whether it was a good investment.

In 1929, Joseph P. Kennedy Sr. was reputed to have been asked for a stock tip by his shoe shine boy. Fearing that speculation in the stock market had reached its zenith, Kennedy was reputed to have sold all his stocks and shorted the market just before the terrible Crash of 1929.

Kennedy made another in a series of fortunes. (That's how the story goes anyway.)

Henderson seems to be getting the same message from the homeless man on the street. When even the destitute are asking for Internet stock tips, hoping to make a quick killing, is it inevitable that the jig is up?

NOTE: By early summer 2000, many Internet stocks had collapsed. Some of the more speculative Internet commerce stocks fell as much as 90 percent! Investors who failed to heed the warnings outlined in the previous chapters saw some magnificent trading profits become substantial investment losses.

8

The Message of the Markets

As I sit at my computer, it is 10:30 A.M., EST, March 17, 2000. Two of the wildest days in Wall Street's colorful history have just passed. In two short days, beginning on the Ides of March, the Dow Industrial Average has surged over 800 points or more than 8 percent, bringing to a close a gut-wrenching correction that lasted exactly two months. In that time, the Dow had fallen 17 percent from its peak of 11,722, reached on January 14. As the Dow had declined in that two month period, the NASDAQ had gone on a tear, gaining 25 percent from the beginning of the year. It closed above the 5000 mark for the first time on March 10, 2000.

The frenetic action in the stock market at the dawn of a new millennium has somewhat muddled the message of the markets. Volatility in stocks and bonds reached historic proportions in the first few months of the year. The major averages moved several hundred points in single days on a routine basis. Interest rates acted erratically. High technology and biotechnology stocks had bigger single-day moves than any market professional can recall witnessing.

One thing seemed clear, however, at the time of this composition. The financial markets were home to the most dynamic economic environment ever known. The struggle between the old, industrial economy and the newest stage of the information age was titanic. The markets, in contractions reminiscent of the birthing process, were sending a message that the world, as we knew it, was changing far too rapidly for many to comprehend.

Entirely new industries were being born, from the Internet to fiber optic networking to genomics. Old industries from automaking to aluminum production to food processing were in danger of being relegated to the dust bin of history. Certainly those industries would not cease to exist, but they may never regain the importance to the economy they once enjoyed.

Appropriately enough, the year 2000 may be home to the most important transition in economic life in human history. Much as the agricultural age gave way to the industrial age, so was the industrial age giving way. Futurists, using the stock market as their guide, boldly proclaimed the coming of a time when the production and transportation of goods and services would be so radically altered by technological innovations that life as we know it would be forever transformed.

Highly efficient means of production, heightened interactivity between producers and consumers, coupled with once unthinkable breakthroughs in modern science, would open the door to longer and better lives for all who inhabit the earth.

That appeared to be the message the financial markets were sending us at the start of a new century. Of course, many said similar things at the turn of the last century. The predictions turned out to be true, but the markets discounted those changes decades before they would be noticed by the person on the street. One can only hope that with the new speed of life, the market's anticipatory mechanisms have much shorter lead times than they did some 100 years ago.

In the summer of 2000, the message of the market had changed decidedly. The once high flying NASDAQ had tumbled a whopping 37 percent from its March 10 high. The Dow and S&P 500 suffered steep corrections as well. Internet and biotech stocks had crashed, many falling between 50 and 90 percent. Bond market interest rates were rising as inflation indicators accelerated to the upside. The yield curve had inverted as the Federal Reserve continued to raise official interest rates. Credit spreads widened. Retail stocks had collapsed.

The market appeared to be warning of an impending recession within a scant few months of promising prosperity forever.

Whether the markets were predicting Paul Samuelson's elusive recession remains to be seen. But in the middle of the year 2000, no one can say that they hadn't been warned or that the message hadn't yet been sent.

Epilogue: The Market Is the Message

The author's fervent hope is that you have come away from this book with a new sense of the markets, how they function, and what they mean. For the last 10 years, Americans have grown preoccupied with market activity, watching the daily ups and downs much as they watch sporting events. The emergence of real-time market information available for free (thanks to CNBC and the Internet) has helped democratize the playing field, giving individual investors information advantages once the sole purview of the professional investor.

Today, the so-called average investor acts much like a professional, ferreting out information about favorite stocks, watching the markets for winners and losers, frequently checking and rebalancing his or her portfolio, and making semieducated guesses about the direction of the stock market, interest rates, or the overall economy.

That's all good news. Americans should be concerned with the markets. They should understand how they work. And they should be compelled to proactively manage their own financial futures.

But simply picking winning stocks or staying abreast of market trends is no longer enough. Individual investors have to do more than just *act* like professionals. They need to *think* like them. By using the markets as a forecasting device, individual investors can take the investment process to a new level of understanding, a level that allows them even more leverage over their futures. This book is not about becoming a more sophisticated market participant just to be smart. It is a means to an end. The deeper your knowledge of the markets, and the more aware you are of the markets' forecasting ability, the less likely it is that you will be blindsided by unforeseen events.

It is the unexpected accident, the "exogenous" event, that changes the course of human affairs. The contents of this book prove that most significant shifts in world history can be accurately anticipated, not by a single vision but through the collective wisdom of the markets.

Some of Wall Street's brightest residents have, many times, ignored the message of the markets. They have suffered the consequences of their folly. You do not have to follow in their footsteps. The markets will always be there to guide your actions, both in good times and in bad. It is incumbent upon you, in order to secure your own future, to let Wall Street be your guide and, most important of all, to listen closely to the message of the markets.

Endnotes

1. Norman C. Miller, *The Great Salad Oil Swindle,* Coward McCann, 1965, p. 12.
2. Ibid., p. 13.
3. Ibid., p. 7.
4. Ibid., p. 245.
5. Ibid., p. 232.
6. Securities and Exchange Commission Study on the Kennedy Assassination and the Markets, November 22, 1963, p. 1.
7. "President Kennedy's Assassination and the Stock Market," New York Stock Exchange Study, p. 3.
8. "Timelines of the Great Depression," compiled from multiple sources, published on The Great Depression home page, March 1999, p. 1.
9. Ibid., p. 2.
10. Ibid., p. 3.
11. Ibid., p. 3.
12. RCA Corporation web page.
13. "The Asian Crisis," an address by Stanley Fischer, first deputy managing director of the International Monetary Fund. Given to the Midwinter Conference of the Bankers' Association for Foreign Trade. January 22, 1998, p. 1.
14. Ibid., p. 1.

15. *Time* magazine cover February 15, 1999.

16. Thomas L. Friedman, "Foreign Affairs," *New York Times,* October 13, 1996.

17. "The Gulf War, a Frontline Chronology" (Internet site), from Rick Atkinson, *Crusade, The Untold Story of the Persian Gulf War,* Houghton Mifflin.

18. *Chronicles,* an interview with Art Cashin, Paine Webber Publication, Fall/Winter 1999.

19. "Chernobyl Commission Report," The Ukranian World Congress, posted by Media Watch Ukraine on the Internet, p. 2.

20. David M. Marples, "Chernobyl Ten Years Later," University of Alberta, Canada, March 21, 1996, posted by Media Watch Ukraine on the Internet, p. 2.

21. "Chernobyl Commission Report," The Ukranian World Congress, posted by Media Watch Ukraine on the Internet, p. 5.

Index